Although the pain of loss is an inevitable part of life, suffering is not. You can heal the pain of your past, and you can grow from this experience in a positive way. Instead of getting worse, your life can and will get better.

Mars and Venus Starting Over is a labor of love. It is my gift to the world and the result of twenty-eight years of serving others like you. I hope it serves you as well during this dark night of the soul. Let it be a little candle in the darkness of your despair. A wise teacher to guide you on your way. An understanding friend to soothe your loneliness. Let it be your companion during this most painful time. Read it again and again and remember you are not alone. Others have been down this road, and they have survived. They have lived to love again. And you will, too!

—from the *Introduction*

Also by John Gray, Ph.D.

Mars and Venus on a Date
Mars and Venus in Love
Mars and Venus Together Forever
Mars and Venus in the Bedroom
What Your Mother Couldn't Tell You
& Your Father Didn't Know
Men Are from Mars, Women Are from Venus
Men, Women and Relationships
What You Feel, You Can Heal

MARS

AND

VENUS

STARTING

OVER

A Practical Guide for Finding Love Again
After a Painful Breakup, Divorce,
or the Loss of a Loved One

John Gray, Ph.D.

HarperPaperbacks
A Division of HarperCollinsPublishers

HarperPaperbacks
A Division of HarperCollins*Publishers*
10 East 53rd Street, New York, NY 10022-5299

ISBN 0-06-109838-8

HarperCollins®, 🔥®, and HarperPaperbacks™ are
trademarks of HarperCollins Publishers, Inc.

Cover design © 1998 by Andrew M. Newman

A hardcover edition of this book was published in 1998 by
HarperCollins*Publishers*.

First HarperPaperbacks printing: August 1999

Printed in the United States of America

Visit HarperPaperbacks on the World Wide Web at
http://www.harpercollins.com

❖ 10 9 8 7 6 5 4 3 2 1

*This book is dedicated
with deepest love and affection
to my soul mate and wife, Bonnie Gray.
Her radiant love continues to bring out
the best in me.*

CONTENTS

x   **Contents**

ACKNOWLEDGMENTS

I thank my wife, Bonnie, for once again sharing the journey of developing a new book.

I thank our three daughters, Shannon, Juliet, and Lauren, for their continued love and support. A special thanks to Helen Drake for efficiently managing my office while I wrote this book.

I thank the following family members and friends for their suggestions and valuable feedback to the ideas in this book: my mother, Virginia Gray; my brothers David, William, Robert, and Tom Gray; my sister, Virginia Gray; Robert and Karen Josephson; Susan and Michael Najarian; Renee Swisko; Ian and Elley Coren; Trudy Green; Candice Fuhrman; Bart and Merril Berens; Martin and Josie Brown; Reggie and Andrea Henkart; Rami El Batrawi; Sandra Weinstein; Robert Beaudry; Jim Puzan; Ronda Coallier; Jim and Anna Kennedy; Alan and Barbara Garber; and Clifford McGuire.

I thank my agent, Patti Breitman, for her continued brilliance and support. I thank my international agent, Linda Michaels, for getting my books published around the world in more than forty languages.

I thank my editor, Diane Reverand, for her expert feedback, direction, and advice. I thank

David Steinberger, president of HarperCollins, and Jane Friedman, CEO, for their guidance and support. I also thank Carl Raymond, Marilyn Allen, Laura Leonard, David Flora, Krista Stroever, and the other incredible staff members at Harper-Collins for their responsiveness to my needs. I could not ask for a better team.

I thank Anne Gaudinier, Rick Harris, John Koroly, and the staff of HarperAudio, and Doug Nichols, Susan Stone, and the staff of Russian Hill Recording who assisted in producing the audio version of the book.

I wish to thank the hundreds of workshop facilitators who teach the Mars Venus Workshops throughout the world, and I thank the thousands of individuals and couples who have participated in my healing workshops over the past fifteen years. I also thank the Mars Venus Counselors who continue to use these principles in their counseling practices.

A very special thanks to my dear friend Kaleshwar.

INTRODUCTION

With the loss of love, our lives are immediately transformed. Starting over, we are suddenly faced with the rest of our lives, and we have no idea what to do. We are stripped of what is most familiar to us with little knowledge of what comes next. Facing this new challenge, we have practically no experience to guide us. Our minds are filled with questions and our hearts with pain. By taking this time to read *Mars and Venus Starting Over,* you will find an abundance of insight and direction. You will know exactly what you need to do and where you are going.

Facing the challenge of starting over, we have no experience to guide us.

The insights in this book come from twenty-eight years of counseling men and women to make wise choices in the process of healing their hearts after a painful breakup, a divorce, or the loss of a loved one. Although their circumstances were unique and widely varied, the pain they felt was the same: the pain of a broken heart. Through counseling and teaching workshops, I have directly assisted thousands of people in the process of healing their hearts.

The insights and processes described in this book have worked repeatedly for them and will work for you. They have also worked for me. In my own life, I have had to start over after a divorce, and I have suffered the loss of my father and my younger brother. I know how devastating a loss can be, and I know the many gifts that come from healing a loss.

After healing the pain from the ending of my first marriage, I was able to learn from my mistakes and go on to create a new and more successful life. Although I would never have thought it then, I am so grateful my first marriage ended. I would have never moved on to marry my wife Bonnie and create the wonderful life and family we now share.

> You will look back to this painful time
> and be grateful for the gifts it brings.

From healing my pain, I was able to create a new life filled with love and success. As my heart opened more fully than ever before, I was able to see things much more clearly. On my healing journey, each day brought new insights and discoveries that prepared me to recognize Bonnie as my soul mate. Successfully giving and receiving love in my marriage and with the encouragement of increasing success in counseling others, I was able to develop the ideas in *Men Are from Mars, Women Are from Venus*.

Through healing my own heart, I became a much better counselor and teacher, but even more important, a better husband and father to my children. Having made the journey from personal experience, I know the incredible rewards of starting over and finding love again.

Even a painful divorce can open the door for you to experience a rich and fulfilling lifetime of love.

This process is not an easy one. To give birth to a new you, to a new life, there are labor pains. It takes hard work. Though at times painful, going through the process is also incredibly rich and fulfilling. After the initial adjustment, it will become much easier. Soon you will be looking back, and all this pain will be just a memory.

Soon all this pain will be just a memory.

Although the death of a loved one is very different from a painful breakup or a divorce, the process of healing our pain is the same. In this book, you will discover how to heal a broken heart regardless of what kind of loss you are suffering. Although you will read stories and examples that are not exactly the same as your situation, you will still probably discover some part of you that relates.

THE THREE PARTS

Mars and Venus Starting Over is divided into three parts. The first part, *Mars and Venus Starting Over*, addresses the part of the healing process that is basically the same for men and women. Although the healing process is the same, men and women often have to confront different challenges. A strategy that is productive for a man is not necessarily productive for a woman, and vice versa.

The second part, Starting Over on Venus, addresses the particular challenges that women face in the process of starting over. The third part, Starting Over on Mars, addresses the unique challenges that men often face. In reading *Mars and Venus Starting Over,* a man may choose to skip part two and then come back to it after reading part three. Both parts contain vital information for both men and women, because there is always some overlap.

Although the process of healing our pain is the same, each of us has many unique challenges to face with our experience of loss. By exploring the insights required to overcome a variety of different situations, you will be able to determine clearly what approach is best for you. Not only will your choices become clearer, but you will find comfort knowing that you are not alone. Others have stood where you stand now, and they have gone forward to find relief and permanent healing.

HEALING OUR HEARTS

On my honeymoon with Bonnie, I received a call informing me of tragic news. My father had been found dead in the trunk of his car. He had been robbed by a hitchhiker and left in the trunk of his car, abandoned by the side of the highway. After a few hours under the hot Texas sun, he died of heat stroke. I, like many others who have lost a loved one, felt the almost unbearable pain and grief of loss. There was no way I could bring him back.

As I continued to grieve, I assumed that this pain could never go away. Fortunately, I was blessed with the support I needed to heal my pain. Now when I think about my father, instead of feeling pain, I feel the sweetness of my love for him and his love for me. Although I wish he were here to enjoy my achievements and to see his grandchildren, there is no pain. As I remember him now, while writing about him, it brings up warm feelings of love and some tears, tears of gratitude for the special times we did spend together.

Even the pain of a tragic loss can
eventually go away.

Two years later, I received another call with more tragic news. My younger brother Jimmy had committed suicide. This world was too cold and harsh for his sensitive soul, and he chose to take his life. Without the knowledge of how to heal his heart after an encounter with drugs and a painful breakup, his life spiraled downward. He became manic-depressive and needed to take medication just to cope. In those days, the medications were not as sophisticated as they are today. The side effects made his life unbearable.

The loss of my brother was devastating. As children, we had been very close. His death was as painful as the loss of my father, but in a different way. Besides missing him, I was so sad that I couldn't help him. I have helped many people, but I could not save him. In grieving his loss, though, I learned to forgive myself.

A big part of our grief is
feeling powerless to save or
bring back our loved one.

Trying to help my brother with his problems was what motivated me to study psychology in the first place. When traditional methods didn't work, I continued searching and expanding my understanding of the healing process.

In facing my feelings of guilt and shame for not saving my brother, I healed my heart once again. This time I discovered a deeper sense of innocence and worthiness. I was able to release the idea that I had to be perfect to be worthy of love. Through healing my pain, I was eventually able to distinguish clearly between feeling responsive to the needs of others and the mistake of feeling responsible for them. These are just a few examples of the gifts I have received from healing my heart after the loss of my brother.

The best gift is that I can continue to feel my love for my brother without a pain in my chest. Instead of feeling pain, I feel grateful that he is no longer in pain. Although I was not able to save him, I have gone on to help many people save themselves. He lives on in my heart, inspiring me to make this world a better place.

MAKING YOUR DREAMS COME TRUE

Millions of people in all walks of life, rich and poor, healthy and sick, continue to suffer from the loss of love. Instead of finding love and making their dreams come true, they are just coping with life. They are trying to get through the day. In most cases, they are not even aware of what they are missing. They don't even know that they have a choice. They don't know that there is a way to heal their hearts and find love again. They don't realize that they can heal their pain.

After reading *Mars and Venus Starting Over*, you will know that you do have a choice. Although the pain of loss is an inevitable part of life, suffering is not. You can heal the pain of your past, and you can grow from this experience in a positive way. Instead of getting worse, your life can and will get better.

Mars and Venus Starting Over is a labor of

love. It is my gift to the world and the result of twenty-eight years of serving others like you. I hope it serves you as well during this dark night of the soul. Let it be a little candle in the darkness of your despair. A wise teacher to guide you on your way. An understanding friend to soothe your loneliness. Let it be your companion during this most painful time. Read it again and again and remember you are not alone. Others have been down this road, and they have survived. They have lived to love again. And you will too!

MARS
AND
VENUS
STARTING
OVER

PART ONE

MARS AND VENUS STARTING OVER

1

MARS AND VENUS STARTING OVER

When single again, men and women face different challenges. Just as we think, feel, and communicate differently, we also respond differently to the loss of love. During a crisis of the heart, a woman's instinctive and automatic reactions are not the same as a man's. Her issues are different as well as her mistakes. What is good for her is not necessarily good for him. In a variety of ways, their needs are worlds apart. It is as if men were from Mars and women were from Venus.

Although we cope differently, both men and women can experience equally agonizing feelings. Starting over after a divorce, a painful breakup, or the death of a loved one can be the most challenging experience of a lifetime. For most people devastated by the loss of love, it is beyond anything we could have expected, predicted, or imagined.

Starting over after a divorce,
a painful breakup, or the death of a
loved one can be the most challenging
experience of a lifetime.

Our hearts ache as they cry out in loneliness and confusion. We are stunned by our helplessness. We fight inside with our inability to change what has happened. We become distraught as we sink into the depths of despair and hopelessness. We feel lost and abandoned in a sea of emptiness and darkness. Time slows down and the passing of each moment seems like eternity.

After a loss, we fight inside ourselves
with our inability to change what has
happened.

It is a struggle simply to fill each empty moment and get through the day. At times the bittersweet pain of loss is replaced by a dull numbness, but then something reminds us of our loss, and once again we long to feel and love again. Never before have we experienced our need for love and connection so agonizingly. As we are forced to face and feel the raw pain in our hearts, we realize our lives will never again be the same.

Eventually, when the healing process is complete, we fully let go. In our minds and hearts, we surrender and accept that we can't change what has happened. Being single again, we start to rebuild our lives. Once more, we begin to reach out to give and receive love. Although we could not have imagined it, our lives come back to a sense of normalcy. After the darkness of despair, the warm, comforting, and soothing sunshine of love reveals itself once again. Although this happy ending is possible, it is not guaranteed.

UNDERSTANDING THE HEALING PROCESS

To heal a broken heart, we must be able to complete the healing process. This requires new insight and understanding, but most people are not aware of what is necessary. We are not taught how to heal a broken heart in school, nor is it something with which we have a lot of practice. Being in the dark and vulnerable, we either blindly follow the advice of friends and family, or we simply follow our own instincts. We make decisions and choices that may sound reasonable but quite often are counterproductive. Though we find temporary relief, in the long run we do not nurture or complete the healing process.

We are not taught how to heal a broken heart in school.

After the loss of love, some people do thrive again. Many are not so successful. After spiraling down to the depths of despair, they never make it out to the other side. To various degrees and in different ways, they continue to suffer their loss. Aware of the pain of losing love, they hold back from fully opening their hearts again.

Others, who appear to have let go, sometimes really haven't. They believe they have successfully moved on, but have done so at the cost of closing the door to their hearts. To avoid feeling their pain, they have moved on too quickly. As a result they have numbed their ability to fully feel. With-

out realizing it or recognizing how they did it, they
have closed up. They carry on in their lives unable
to feel the love in their hearts. Their ability to grow
in love and happiness is stunted.

Becoming single again is definitely a crisis. Like
any crisis, it is a time of danger and a time of
opportunity. The opportunity is the possibility of
healing and strengthening your heart and mind so
that you will move on healthy and whole. The
danger is that you do not complete the healing
process. Time alone does not heal all wounds.
How we cope with the loss of love determines the
rest of our lives.

HOW THE HEART HEALS

To ensure that we complete the healing process, it
is important that we understand the basics of how
the heart heals. This process is most easily understood and visualized by considering how a broken
bone heals. An emotional wound is abstract, but a
broken bone is very tangible and concrete. Recognizing the various steps in healing a broken bone
can assist us in acknowledging and respecting the
needs of our broken heart.

When a bone breaks, our body already contains
the natural healing power to correct the problem.
It hurts, but eventually the pain goes away. As long
as we don't interfere, the body heals itself automatically, in a predictable time period. When this
automatic healing process is allowed and nurtured, the bone will actually grow back stronger

than before. In a similar way, if you are able to nurture the healing of a broken heart, it also will grow back stronger. The pain and despair will pass, and you will find love and joy again.

When a broken heart heals it actually
grows back stronger.

When a bone is broken, it must be reset and then be protected in a cast to allow the body's automatic and natural healing processes to occur. If the bone is not reset straight, then it will grow back crooked. If it is not given enough time to rest, protected in a cast, it will remain weak. Likewise, if the protective cast is never taken off, the bone will never fully become strong again. Similar warnings apply to the process of healing a broken heart.

When our hearts are broken, it is not enough simply to assume that we will get over it. Although the healing is automatic, without an understanding of the complete process it is quite possible and even common to interfere and obstruct the healing unknowingly. Using the analogy of healing a broken bone, we can begin to recognize and appreciate the three essential steps to healing a broken heart.

The three steps for healing a broken bone are: getting help, resetting the bone, and then giving it time to heal by protecting the bone in a cast. In a similar way, the three steps for healing the heart are:

Step One:	Getting help
Step Two:	Grieving the loss
Step Three:	Becoming whole before getting involved again

Let's explore this analogy in greater depth.

THE THREE STEPS FOR HEALING THE HEART

Step One: Getting Help

After breaking a bone, the first step is to get help. When you are wounded, you require the support of others. Even if you were an expert in setting bones, you would still find another expert to assist you. Likewise, when your heart is broken, the first and most important step is to get help. This is not the time to be stoic and push away your feelings of hurt and loss. Men can speed up their healing process by hearing from others who are in pain, while women particularly benefit from being heard. Sharing your feelings and spending time with people who know what you are going through is not only comforting but is essential to the healing process.

Men can speed up their healing process by hearing from others who are in pain, while women particularly benefit from being heard.

Although reading this book is definitely a good beginning, it still does not replace your need for support from people who are experiencing a similar loss or have already been through it. If you were ever to take a workshop, join a support group, or seek help from a counselor, this would be the best time. The support of others who have healed emotional wounds and the assistance of a trained expert can ensure that you have the opportunity to heal completely. During a healing crisis, you are actually most receptive to what a counselor, support group, or workshop can offer you.

Throughout *Mars and Venus Starting Over*, we will explore the various ways men and women unknowingly push away the very love and support that is required to complete the healing process. In addition, we will focus on practical strategies for getting the support you need. Although there is no immediate way to take away the pain, you *can* get the necessary support to make it bearable. With the right help and at the right time, you will release your pain and experience the joy and peace of an open heart once again.

Step Two: Grieving the Loss

In the second step, after seeking help, the bone must be put back the way it was before the break. By resetting the bone, it then has the opportunity to grow back straight. Likewise, when your heart is broken, it must be put back the way it was before. In this second stage, we must take time to grieve the loss by remembering the person and what happened in the relationship.

After the loss of a loved one, remembering your past together brings up painful feelings, but it also evokes the love you shared. Reexperiencing this love helps you to heal. This love soothes and heals the pain of loss.

By feeling gratitude for the good times and forgiveness for the mistakes, the heart is filled with the love it needs to heal itself.

If you are healing from a painful breakup or a divorce and you feel rejected and betrayed, then it may, at first, be hard to grieve the loss or feel the love. You may be too angry. In this case, the challenge of "resetting the heart" is to find forgiveness. Then you will be able to grieve fully.

Even when you are glad and relieved to end a relationship that was abusive, your challenge is to go back to remember your initial hopes and dreams, and then to grieve that disappointment. After parting ways, in order to reset your heart, you must seek to appreciate what was good and to forgive the mistakes. This process sets you free to move on with an open heart to find true and lasting love.

It is impossible for your heart to open fully to another when it is completely closed to someone in your past.

As a result of resetting our hearts by fully grieving, we are once again able to feel the tender, innocent, and delicate desire in our hearts to care for another and to trust another's love. Without this healing, we may become too jaded to care or to trust once more.

Until the healing process is complete, men tend to stop caring as much, while women have problems with trusting again. As a result, men may get involved right away, but they have trouble committing. On the other hand, women will tend to avoid getting hurt again by not getting involved.

Until the healing process is complete,
men have trouble making a
commitment and women have
problems with trusting again.

In subsequent chapters, we will explore in great detail how to grieve a loss successfully and to feel our emptiness fully, so that we can fill up with love. Just as light follows the darkness of the night, the fullness of love rushes in to fill us up when we fully experience our inner emptiness.

Step Three: Becoming Whole

In the third step of healing a broken bone, after resetting the bone, we must then protect it in a cast and give it time to heal. Once it is strong again, it is time to take off the cast. In a similar way, in the process of healing the heart, we must take time to become whole before getting involved intimately. Before we can successfully share with another, we must heal our neediness and have a strong sense of self. The best time to get involved again is when you feel as if you don't have to. Ideally, we must be generally fulfilled and complete before entering into another intimate relationship.

The best time to get involved again is when you feel as if you don't have to.

Men commonly get involved too soon, while women will unknowingly push away love. Unless we take the necessary time before getting involved again, men will be restricted in their ability to give of themselves, while women are restricted in their ability to receive love. In later chapters, we will explore in great detail how men and women unknowingly sabotage this third stage and will examine practical suggestions for making sure you get involved again at the right time.

STARTING OVER

Being single again, our lives are suddenly transformed. It is as though we are suddenly faced with the rest of our lives and have no idea what to do. We are stripped of what is most familiar to us and often have no idea what to do. By taking this time to read *Mars and Venus Starting Over*, you will find that insight and direction.

2

WHY DOES IT HURT SO MUCH?

Of all losses, the loss of love is most painful. When we suffer other disappointments and injustices, it is love that comforts the soul and makes our pain bearable. In our daily lives, when we experience loss, rejection, or failure, our minds automatically protect us by remembering that at home we are loved. But when love is lost, there is no way to find relief; there is no comfort or protection. Most often we are not aware of how much we rely on this support until it is taken away.

When we suffer disappointments and injustices, it is love that comforts the soul and makes our pain bearable.

When we lose a primary source of love, we are suddenly stripped of all our defenses and forced to experience the raw pain of loss, the hurt of deprivation, and the sadness of loneliness. At this point, we not only mourn the loss of our loved one, but we pray for relief and ask, "Why does it hurt so much?"

There is no way we could ever anticipate the agonizing pain and emptiness following the loss of love. Whether we have experienced a painful breakup, a divorce, or the tragic death of a loved one, the result is a broken heart. At first we are stunned. We feel a sudden numbness. Every cell in our body exclaims, "No! It can't be. I won't let it. This is not happening." As we cry out to God, we refuse to accept the loss.

We hope that we can wake up the next day and everything will be back to normal. If only it could be a bad dream. Soon, we realize it *has* happened, and we can't go back to change it. When we accept our helplessness, reality sets in, and we begin to feel alone. Looking out at the horizon of our life, it is cold and barren. As our numbness gradually thaws, we realize that we are in pain, and it hurts a lot.

It is not easy to let go or to say good-bye to someone we love; we are too attached. To find relief and heal our broken heart, we must first understand the nature of love, dependence, and attachment.

LOVE, DEPENDENCE, AND ATTACHMENT

When there is someone to greet us at the end of the day, someone to appreciate what we do, someone who recognizes our worth and benefits from our existence, it gives our life meaning and purpose. We are happiest when someone cares for us, makes us feel special and important, understands our sorrows, and celebrates our successes. As we grow in love, we naturally become more dependent on our partner for love.

Even if we are not always getting what we want and need, the hope of getting what we need and the effort to make a relationship work will also increase our dependence. Even if the love we share is not always idyllic, the hope of being loved will still buffer us from the cold, uncaring, indifferent world outside the relationship. In a multitude of ways, when we love someone, we depend more and more on his or her presence.

As this dependence grows, an important change takes place. Over time, we stop feeling our basic need to love and be loved; instead we begin to feel a more specific need—the need to love and be loved by *our partner*. We stop feeling our general need for love, but feel a new need: our partner's love. No one else will do. This shift is called *attachment*. From depending on our partners for love, we gradually become attached to *their* love.

In a love relationship, we replace
our need for love with the need
for our partner's love.

When we are attached to a spouse, it is not enough to be appreciated by others. For appreciation to be most meaningful, it must be from our partner. It does not carry the same weight when someone else gives us a compliment or listens to our problems. Throughout the day, we give and receive in a variety of ways, but the exchanges don't provide the same degree of fulfillment as when our partner is involved.

When we lose a loved one, to the degree that we are attached, we are emotionally convinced that we will never love again. We feel that without our spouse's love, we cannot get what we need to be happy and for our lives to be meaningful. This sense of hopelessness magnifies the pain of our loss a hundred times. It is one thing to feel that you will have to go without food for a day, but it is completely different to believe that you will never eat again. When we lose something that seems irreplaceable, it is a devastating experience.

Attachment magnifies our pain a hundred times.

To heal our broken heart, we must release our attachment and open ourselves to giving and receiving love with others. If we do not take the risk to open our heart again, we will either stay stuck in our pain or remain emotionally numb. The process of letting go of our attachment allows us to reset our heart and move on.

Resetting our heart allows us to feel our basic need for love once again. Instead of specifically needing our partner's love, we begin to feel our general need for love. By letting go, we can gradually reexperience the openness we felt before we became attached. We are no longer dependent on our partner's love, but open to other sources of love and support.

Contained within this unattached openness is the intuitive knowledge of where we can find love. By letting go of the attached desire for our partner's love and feeling our soul's need to love and be loved, we discover that within the awareness of our need is the unfolding knowledge and power to find its fulfillment. Until we are able to let go of our attachment, we are not able to tap into this innate ability to find love.

> Contained within the awareness
> of our soul's need for love is the
> intuitive knowledge and power
> to find its fulfillment.

Letting go of a partner is difficult to the degree that we are dependent on him. As we are able to get what we need from our family and friends, our dependence on our partner lessens. As we gradually fill up with love without depending on our partner, we are able to release our pain *completely*.

In other words, by opening ourselves to giving and receiving without depending on our partner, we can eventually let go. As we fill up with new love and share that love, the emptiness disappears. Although the love we give and receive is certainly not the same, our new love gradually becomes equally fulfilling.

THE ART OF LETTING GO

Starting over requires developing the skill of letting go. To move on, we must once again feel our innate need for love without our partner to fulfill that need. To accomplish this end, we must be very skillful, otherwise, instead of letting go, we may unknowingly increase our attachment.

If I am holding onto something, and you try to pull it away, my tendency is to fight and struggle. I will hold on even tighter than before. This is what happens when we are attached. We don't want to let go, and as a result we hold on even more tightly.

The secret for letting go of an attachment is to go with the flow. Don't try to let go. Instead, keep holding on. Remember how much you love your partner, feel how much you want your partner, feel how much you need your partner, feel your gratitude for all the gifts your partner has given you, feel how much you wish you could bring back your partner.

The secret for letting go of an attachment is to go with the flow. Don't try to let go.

By remembering your partner in this way, you are grieving properly. This is how the healing takes place. In the beginning, by remembering your partner, you will feel the loss even more intensely. You may experience a variety of painful feelings: anger, sadness, fear, and sorrow. Feeling these different painful emotions is actually how we release an attachment. This pain is temporary.

Eventually, after releasing your attachment, you may still feel some sorrow when you remember your partner. You will also feel the sweetness of your love and the strength of your spirit. When your heart is fully healed, remembering your partner is no longer painful; instead, it becomes a special way to connect with the everlasting love you share deep in your soul.

At this point, when you think of your partner your heart is filled with love and peace. This experience is the signal that you are ready to get involved again. It provides a basis that ensures you will be fully capable of finding true and lasting love.

When your heart is fully healed,
remembering your partner is
no longer painful. Instead, it evokes
the sweetness of your love.

To heal our broken hearts, we need first to face and feel the painful emotions that come up. This healing process occurs automatically as long as we keep remembering our partner. By actively creating opportunities to remember our loss, we are actually evoking the love we need to accept the loss and to let go.

In various cultures and religious traditions, taking time to feel grief is nurtured. A variety of rituals of remembrance are recommended. For example: Dress in black for a period of time, burn a long-lasting candle, plant a tree, tell stories at the funeral, revisit the grave site with love offerings, pass down a family heirloom, put up special pictures. In each instance, we can see the common thread. By taking time to remember our partner with love, we give ourselves the opportunity to heal.

FINDING LOVE AGAIN

After the death of a spouse or loved one, painful feelings emerge because a part of us believes we will never love again. Without the alive, physical presence of our partner to love, we stop loving. Our heart caves in and we are engulfed by pain.

Our heart caves in not because we have
lost love, but because we have
temporarily stopped loving.

Even after a divorce, this same process occurs. Our ex-partner may still be alive, but the relationship we had hoped to have is gone. The person with whom we planned to share our life is no longer present in our lives. For the purpose of grieving and letting go, it is as if they have died. The loss we feel after a divorce can be as real as after the death of a spouse.

Without the physical presence of our partner, we believe that we cannot love or be loved. Although this belief is not true, it takes time to adjust and correct. It is not easily discarded. For years, we have depended on our partner's physical presence to trigger our love. Our daily experience has been that their presence has been the target of our love and a tangible source of support. It takes time to release this attachment and discover that we can continue to love them.

When a partner is gone, we are forced to feel our love without them. We cannot touch them or feel their arms around us, but we can remember how wonderful it felt. We can remember their love, feel their support, and continue to give our love to them.

**Although we will never see
our partner again, they live on
forever in our hearts.**

In the grieving process, we eventually discover that the love in our hearts continues on, not dependent on our partner's presence. Our future is not as gloomy as we thought. As the knowledge that we can continue loving shifts from a concept to our daily experience, we find peace. The gray clouds of despair disappear, revealing the warm sunshine of love. We accept our loss, but we do not forget. A gentle breeze blows our hair back as we set out on our new journey. Starting over, we feel confident that we will find the love we deserve. We are inspired to share the special love we feel deep in our hearts.

3

EMOTIONAL LAG TIME

Long before the heart is ready to let go, the mind wants to move on. This speedy thinking is fine for the mind, but it is not the way the heart heals. The heart moves much more slowly. This difference can be compared to light and sound. For the sake of analogy, if the mind moves at the speed of light, then, in comparison, the heart moves at the speed of sound. There is a significant difference.

In the physical world, we can objectively observe the difference between the speeds of light and sound. We don't question it because we can physically measure these different speeds. It is much harder to observe the mental and emotional world. Although we don't commonly see or measure the mind and heart, we must recognize the difference to heal a broken heart successfully.

When we lose love, it takes a lot longer for our heart to adjust than for the mind. As soon as we think we are ready to move on, another wave of painful feelings comes up. This ebb and flow of feelings is not only natural, but a necessary process. The heart does not let go in one step, but rather gradually and in waves, just as the tides our unresolved feelings come and go. At low tide, not only does the pain go away, but we discover one more degree of the power and knowledge within ourselves to find love once again. Then the high tide comes and we are flooded with unresolved feelings of anger, sadness, fear, and sorrow. Through this process of grieving again and again, we eventually let go and find love.

At low tide, we may feel that everything is fine. In our minds, we have adjusted to the loss, and we are ready to move on. When high tide comes in we are suddenly facing our unresolved feelings again. One day you are optimistic and ready to move on, but then the next day you feel angry, sad, or afraid. While this may seem a little crazy, it is not. Just as light and sound travel at different speeds, the mind and heart change, adjust, adapt, and self-correct at different speeds. In the healing process, it is normal and even healthy for feelings to lag behind the mind.

It is normal and even healthy for feelings to lag behind the mind in the healing process.

THE RULES OF SURVIVAL

Most people are tempted to move on before the healing process is complete. After all, no one likes pain. It is only natural to want out of it as soon as possible. Avoiding painful circumstances is a healthy approach to life. The most important rule of "survival" is to avoid pain and seek out pleasure. So, when painful feelings come up, the mind says, "Okay, enough is enough. Why does it take so long? Let's move on!" Under normal circumstances this tendency is good, but during a healing crisis it can make matters worse.

Without the knowledge and insight into how to process and move beyond our negative feelings, our emotions can become unbearable. To find relief we seek to escape our feelings of loss. By moving out of our feelings too soon, we unknowingly sabotage the healing process. We make decisions and plans that bring short-term relief but are counterproductive in the long run. This tendency to avoid and to resist painful feelings is the very thing that can cause various degrees of depression.

Resisting painful feelings can cause
various degrees of depression.

When we resist the reoccurring waves of anger, hurt, anxiety, emptiness, and loneliness, we may experience temporary relief, but we are unable to let go. Despite our efforts to rise above these feelings, they grip our awareness and pull us back down. Without a clear and positive understanding of the healing process, we may easily become stuck in despair. As depression and hopelessness set in, it may even seem as if there's no way out. As a result, we seek to avoid our feelings even more fervently. This self-defeating cycle can only be stopped by taking the necessary time to heal our hearts.

Despite our efforts to rise above painful feelings, they grip our awareness and pull us back down.

Even if you are the one to end a relationship, it is still perfectly normal and healthy to experience feelings of grief and loss. After a breakup, your mind may say, "But it's a good thing that this relationship ended. Now I have the opportunity to find real love and support." Although this is true and the mind is ready to move on, the heart may be saying things like, "I feel so sad, I feel so alone. I don't know if I will ever be loved. I may never be happy again."

A resolved mind is the first step. The second and lengthier step is to explore and release unresolved feelings. Taking extra time to examine the feelings is not only normal but also healthy. It allows the healing to be complete.

When the mind is resolved, it believes once again, "All is okay. Life is what it is, and it is all right." This positive and clear resolution in the mind provides a strong basis to process and release the unresolved feelings in the heart. An objective but positive point of view assists the heart in letting go.

> When the mind is resolved,
> it believes once again, "All is okay.
> Life is what it is, and it is all right."

Unfortunately, many people are not aware of this process. When the mind has taken the time it needs to adjust or adapt itself to the new situation, they become impatient with the feelings of the heart and want to move on too quickly. This tendency to rush the process is common to both men and women, yet we do it in different ways. Let's first explore how women commonly do it.

HOW WOMEN AVOID THE PAIN OF LOSS

A woman's tendency to avoid the pain of loss and to find relief is most commonly accomplished by denying her need for love. She protects herself from feeling her pain by deciding not to trust or depend on love again. On Venus, they are very relationship oriented. Their greatest pain is to feel abandoned. It is unbearable to feel dependent on another and then have him not be there. When a woman doesn't recognize the importance of exploring her feelings, she will either bury her pain by giving too much to others or she will pull back from intimate relationships and become overly self-reliant.

> A woman's tendency to avoid pain
> and seek relief is accomplished by
> denying her need for love.

Being overly self-reliant means she behaves as if she doesn't need others for comfort and support. She may particularly resist getting intimately involved. Certainly, some time is needed before getting involved again, but to avoid the possible pain of abandonment she will minimize the importance of an intimate relationship. She may tell herself that it is not that important for her. By denying the importance of her need for intimacy, she is then able to avoid experiencing the ongoing feelings of loss.

Giving too much means she makes the needs of others more important than her own needs. This can be another approach to avoid feeling her own needs. By feeling and responding to the needs of others, she finds temporary relief. For example, by getting involved in giving to her children, a charity, or a cause, she is temporarily able to escape her own emptiness and pain. Serving others is certainly a good thing, but, particularly for women healing a broken heart, it can be a way to avoid experiencing and releasing their own unresolved feelings.

To move out of her pain,
a woman will either begin giving too
much to others or she will pull back
from intimate relationships.

Once we have been burned, even the thought of getting near a fire can bring up the fear of being burned again. Likewise, even the remote possibility of becoming attached can bring up unresolved feelings and issues. By deciding not to trust again, a woman is able to distance herself from feeling hurt, abandoned, and betrayed. By planning not to get involved, she does not have to confront her fears of being hurt again or feel her grief from having been hurt.

Let's look at some of the feelings that may come up after the loss of love and then explore how the mind reacts to push them away. While these attempts of the mind are reasonable and loving gestures, they do not help heal a broken heart.

HOW A WOMAN'S MIND AND HEART REACT DIFFERENTLY

When the heart feels:	Her mind thinks:
I feel so frustrated being alone. I have to do everything. I want so much to feel loved and supported.	You have to accept reality. If you want something, then you have to do it yourself. This is what happens when you need others.
I feel so discouraged. I am so alone. No one understands. No one really cares about me. If only I could turn back clock.	You don't need love that much anyway. You have given so much, now it is your turn. You can take care of yourself. It's time to move on. You can make a new life.

I feel worried that I will never find love again. No one will ever make me happy. I feel so powerless; there is nothing I can do.

You can learn to make yourself happy. It's not healthy to be so dependent on others. Try giving to others; that will make you happy.

I feel embarrassed that I am alone and unattached. Why? Why? What did I do? Is something so wrong with me? Am I so unlovable?

Just hold your head high. You don't have to show how you feel. Don't break down. Keep it together, and then you will not be a burden to others.

I feel angry that I am not loved and supported in my life. It is not right. I deserve more. If this is the way it is, then I don't want to love again.

You expect too much from life. Nothing lasts forever. This is the time to let go. Make sure you take care of yourself.

I feel so sad. I will never love again. My life feels so empty. There is a big hole in my heart that can never be filled.

You shouldn't say things like that. Think about all the good things in your life. Think about all the other people who love you. It could be much worse.

I feel afraid I will never find the right person. I will always be alone. I will never taste the sweetness of love or feel its strong arms around me.

That's why you need to learn to take care of yourself. You don't need anyone else. You have to be strong.

I feel sorry that my life has turned out this way. I feel so bad. I wish I could make it different. My life is so barren.

Try thinking about others and not yourself. Keep busy. As long as you keep busy, then you will be fine.

I feel furious. I can't believe this has happened. It is outrageous. It is not fair. I will not be treated this way.

You expect too much from relationships. Just take care of yourself. Don't be so needy, then you will never be so vulnerable.

I feel so hurt. I trusted your love. I feel so abandoned. How could you leave me? You hurt me so much. You promised always to love me.

It hurts too much to lose love. You should be more careful before you become attached, then you will never be hurt again. You trust too much.

I feel scared of being alone. I don't know how to function this way. It is so painful.

You can survive without being with a partner. It is not so bad. At least you will not be abandoned again.

I feel ashamed. I should have been more loving. Maybe this would not have happened. Things could have been different. I feel so unworthy.

These feelings are not good for you. You have to start loving yourself and get on with your life. There is so much to do. Other people have it worse than you do.

In each of the examples above, the heart is feeling the loss, but the mind is ready to move on. The resolved mind uses reason to hurry the heart. If a woman is to heal a broken heart, she has to be careful of this tendency to find immediate relief. Instead she must decisively allow herself to take time for herself and to open up to receive support from others. This is not the time for her to take care of others, but the time to prioritize her needs. This is not the time to pull back from established relationships, but the time to reach out and to let others be there for her.

HOW MEN AVOID THE PAIN OF LOSS

On Mars, the population is very solution oriented. If there is pain, a man's priority is to do what he can do to get rid of that pain. When a man does not understand this need to take time before moving on, he will either avoid or minimize his feelings by becoming overly engaged in work, or he will rush right into another relationship to soothe his wounds.

To speed up the process, a man will
either bury his feelings in work or
soothe his wounds by rushing into
another exclusive relationship.

This explains why many men tend to move on very quickly from one relationship to another. If his problem is the loss of love, then he solves that problem by finding love again. When he rushes into another relationship right away, his actions do not mean he did not love the woman with whom he was previously involved. His behavior is in no way a reflection of how much he cared. He is just seeking to get out of his pain. In some cases, the greater the loss, the more quickly he may try to be involved in another relationship. This automatic tendency can be counterproductive.

When a man rushes into another relationship, his behavior is not a reflection of how much he cared for his previous partner.

Most men do not have an instinctive understanding of how to heal the heart. Much of the Martian philosophy is good for solving problems, but not great for a broken heart. A man does not instinctively know that bringing up his feelings again and again is an essential part of the healing process. To succeed in healing a broken heart a man has to guide his instincts with higher reason, insight, and wisdom.

He must be careful to restrain himself from making a new commitment right away. Certainly it is fine if he chooses to find comfort in an intimate relationship as long as he and his new partner recognize that he is on the rebound. After a few months of healing, his feelings may change quickly. It is, therefore, not advisable for him to make any promises or commitments. To avoid leading a woman on, it is best for him to be dating two or more partners. To become attached to one partner interferes with the healing process of letting go.

When the mind is resolved, there are a variety of ways men may unknowingly resist the natural healing process of the heart. Let's look at some of the formulas that work to solve problems, but don't work to heal the heart. In the following chart, we will explore some feelings of the heart that get discounted or minimized by the mind. Although these statements of the mind are certainly reasonable, see if you can sense how they push away the feelings that still may need to be felt. Women may relate to these examples as well. Remember, every person, man or woman, has a masculine and feminine side. Regardless of your gender, you may relate in various degrees to the male and female charts.

HOW A MAN'S MIND AND HEART REACT DIFFERENTLY

When the heart feels:	The mind thinks:
I feel so frustrated. I hate this. This is painful and hard. I feel so empty.	Just bite the bullet and move on. This isn't the end of the world.
I feel so discouraged; I don't know what to do. I feel like just giving up.	You can't change the way things are. You just should just accept reality and move on.

I feel so worried. Things will never be the same. My life is ruined. Nothing is working out.	You shouldn't worry so much about it. Just take each day as it comes and do what you have to do.
I feel so embarrassed. I feel like such a failure. I don't know how I can ever show my face in public. I feel so inadequate.	Look, these things happen. Now pick yourself up and get out there. You can get what you want.
I am so angry this has happened. It's not right, and I will not stand for it. This will never happen again.	Life's just not fair. So forget it. You don't need anyone, just take care of yourself. There are more fish in the sea. It's not the end of the world.
I can't bear this pain. I am so sad. I feel so alone and abandoned. There is nothing anymore to make me happy.	How much longer are you going to keep this up? You are only making it worse. Count your blessings.
I am afraid I'll never find love again. Now I have to start over. I have lost so much. What if it just gets worse?	You are making too much of this. It's not such a big deal. Let it go and get on with your life.
I feel so bad. I am so sorry. If only I had done it differently. Oh, please, give me another chance.	Hey, nobody's perfect. There is nothing you can do about it now. Give yourself a break and move on.

I feel furious this has happened. It's not right. I can't believe it.

What do you care? just take care of yourself from now on. Who needs the grief?

I feel so hurt. You promised. You said you would always love me. How could you leave?

Come on, don't be a baby. Grow up. You can handle this. Get going.

I feel so scared. It is hopeless. I'll never be hapy again. This can't be happening.

What's done is done. You can't carry on like forever. You have to just accept it.

I feel so ashamed. I should never have allowed this to happen.

That's the way the cards were dealt. Don't whine about it, fix it.

In each of the examples above, it is easy to see how the mind can invalidate the feelings of the heart. Some of the examples may express not only what your mind is thinking, but also what some of your friends are saying to you. Your friends may feel compassion for you, but after seeing you suffer for a few weeks, they may also rush you to move on. Although they mean well, their advice can be counterproductive.

Your friends may feel compassion for you, but after seeing you suffer for a few weeks, they want you to move on.

They think, as your own mind does, that you're making it worse by taking so long to heal. They may think you are being self-indulgent. From their perspective, you can't continue to cry over spilt milk forever. They don't realize that these recurring feelings are coming up for a very good reason.

When your mind is ready to accept the
loss and move on, your heart needs at
least several months more.

With the correct approach and enough time, you will eventually be able to dispel the darkness of despair and find the light of love and joy in your heart once again. It is important to recognize the consequences of not devoting enough time to healing. Even if a relationship was unloving and unsupportive, we still have to heal our heart when it ends. In the next chapter, we will explore the issues and challenges associated with grieving the loss of love.

4

GRIEVING THE LOSS OF LOVE

Grieving the loss of love means fully feeling and then releasing all the painful emotions that come up when we reflect on our loss. Although this is an automatic process, there are many ways we can interfere unknowingly. As the previous chapter explains, one common mistake is to move on too quickly, not giving ourselves enough time to grieve. Yet another mistake is not giving ourselves permission to experience all our feelings.

When we lose a partner or a relationship ends, we expect to feel waves of sadness and sorrow, but this is only a part of the grieving process. To release our attachment to a person or relationship, other feelings need to be experienced and released.

THE FOUR HEALING EMOTIONS

To release our attachment, we need to experience four healing emotions: anger, sadness, fear, and sorrow. As long as we continue to feel angry or sad, we are still attached in some way. If we feel fear and sorrow, we are not yet open to the new possibilities that exist for us. Each of these four healing emotions is vitally important if we are to let go and to move on. They play an essential role in the process of releasing attachment and "resetting" our hearts.

Just as a broken bone needs to be reset to heal correctly, our desires must also be reset. Instead of continuing to look in one direction for our wants and needs, we must reset our direction to open ourselves to new sources of love and support. Exploring and feeling the four healing emotions frees us to adjust our wants, expectations, needs, and hopes. Each of these four primary healing emotions plays an important role. Let's examine and explore the significance of each.

HEALING EMOTION 1: ANGER

Anger allows us to explore emotionally what has happened that we didn't want to happen. Anger is the emotional recognition that we are not getting what we want. It is an alarm signal that commands us to stop and to adjust ourselves to what has happened. After a loss, unless we give ourselves permission to be angry, we may remain stuck in a numb, lifeless, and passionless state. Feeling anger breaks us free from indifference and reconnects us to our passion for love and life.

Feeling then releasing anger reconnects
us to our passion for love and life.

As a result of feeling anger, we are able to release our attachments to our past wants and to begin to feel new wants and desires free of attachment. When desire is free of attachment, we are open to all possibilities. Instead of "I want my partner's love," the need becomes "I want to be loved." Contained within unattached desire is the intuitive ability to recognize new and appropriate sources of love and support.

HEALING EMOTION 2: SADNESS

Sadness allows us to emotionally explore what did not happen that we wanted to happen. Sadness is the emotional recognition of what we wanted to happen that didn't. After a loss, unless we give ourselves permission to be sad, we cannot adjust our expectations to what is now possible. Feeling sadness reconnects us to our ability to love, value, and enjoy what we do have. While anger gradually renews our passion for life, sadness opens our hearts to feel the sweetness of love once again.

Feeling and then releasing sadness
opens our hearts to feel the sweetness
of love once again.

As a result of feeling sadness, we are able to surrender up our resistance to what has happened and gradually to accept the loss. This surrender provides the basis for adjusting our expectations. Going back and feeling the various nuances of what we wanted to happen is essential if we are to reset our expectations. Instead of "I expect my partner's love," our need becomes "I expect to be loved." Contained within this unattached expectation is the unfolding confidence and self-assurance that we can get what we want.

HEALING EMOTION 3: FEAR

Fear allows us to explore what could happen that we do not want to happen. Fear is not a prediction of doom, but an emotional recognition of what we do not want to happen. Feeling fear and our resistance to what could happen reconnects us to our vulnerability. That reconnection provides the ability to discern what we need and can depend on now. It assists us to open up to receive the support we need and fills our hearts with courage and gratitude.

Feeling and then releasing fear
provides the ability to discern what we
need and can depend on now.

As a result of feeling our fears, we are able to adapt our needs to what is available now instead of continuing to need what is no longer ours.

Instead of "I need my partner's love and support," our need becomes "I need to be loved and supported." Contained within this unattached need is the power and determination necessary to find love again.

HEALING EMOTION 4: SORROW

Sorrow allows us to explore what cannot happen that we want to happen. Sorrow is the emotional recognition that what we want to happen cannot be. This awareness is crucial to letting go of an attachment. Sorrow is an acknowledgment of our powerlessness to undo what has happened. By reflecting on *what is not possible* we shift to our ability to discern *what is possible*. This ability assists us in receiving the compassion necessary to heal our wounds and eventually provides the inspiration to give the love in our heart once again. Ultimately, the emotional resignation of sorrow brings us peace.

Feeling and then releasing sorrow
provides the ability to discern
what is possible.

As a result of feeling sorrow, we are able to release our past hopes and eventually find new hope. Instead of "I wish my partner was here to love me," our need becomes "I hope to be loved." Contained within this unattached hope is the intention and motivation required to start over once again. Until the light of new hope begins to emerge, we cannot fully experience the flow of love once again within our hearts. As hope dawns, we begin to feel released from the darkness of our despair.

Each of the four healing emotions plays an essential part in the process of healing a broken heart. One is not better than the other, nor is there a particular order in which we should feel them. Quite often, after a loss or disappointment, we will experience first the anger, then sadness, then fear, and finally sorrow. Yet in different situations and with different people, the healing emotions come up in a different order.

Being aware of all four healing emotions assists us in fully exploring our feelings to heal our hurt. When even one emotion is neglected, it can delay or even obstruct the healing process. To grieve the loss of love properly, we need to make sure that in our mind we give our heart permission to feel each of the four healing emotions.

NEGATIVE EMOTIONS HELP US TO CHANGE DIRECTIONS

If we are driving a car in one direction and decide to stop to turn around, we have to apply the brakes. Feeling the four healing emotions resembles the process of putting on the brakes before we can turn around. The mind recognizes we have to change directions, but it is the role of the heart to put on the brakes. In order to change directions and love again, we must first stop holding on and let go in our hearts.

Grieving our loss is a process of letting go that frees us to change directions and assists us to update our wants, expectations, needs, and hopes. As we stop depending on our partner's love, which is no longer available, we are able to open up to receive the abundance of love that is available.

When we are no longer dependent on
our partner's love, we are open to
receiving what is available.

We cannot release an attachment and move on unless we first become aware of it. Emotional pain signals that we are still holding on to what is no longer available. Feeling the pain associated with each of the four healing emotions eventually triggers a release from pain. If someone tossed you a hot potato, you would automatically toss it away. In a similar way, when we are fully able to experience the pain of holding on, we automatically let go. By experiencing the healing emotions, the pain diminishes and we are eventually able to fully let go.

When we are fully able to experience
the pain of holding on, then we
automatically let go.

If we are unable to experience the complete range of our feelings, we can become stuck at any one level. Instead of feeling our emotions and then finding relief, we end up stuck in negative feelings. Being stuck means that no matter how much we feel an emotion it doesn't go away. Instead of letting go we eventually become numb; instead of opening our hearts to new opportunities for love and happiness, we close up.

Instead of feeling our emotions
and then finding relief, we can get
stuck in negative feelings.

To complete the grieving process each of the four healing emotions must be fully experienced. Most people, unaware of this dynamic, unfortunately never complete the healing process. When they lose love, they experience one or two healing emotions, but not all four. Instead of moving on, they become stuck. In the next chapter, we will explore how to make sure you don't get stuck in any on feeling, but instead move on to experience increasing love, happiness, and peace.

5

GETTING UNSTUCK

This new insight about the four healing emotions explains why just getting in touch with feelings does not always work. Sometimes, dipping into our feelings results in our getting stuck. Instead of feeling better, we end up feeling worse. As with quicksand, the more we struggle to get out of our emotional pain, the deeper we sink.

After a few experiences like this, we do everything in our power to avoid feeling our negative emotions. In the short run, we may avoid or minimize our emotional pain, but this temporary relief comes with a hidden cost.

By suppressing or numbing negative
emotions, we gradually lose our ability
to feel positive emotions.

One of the reasons it is so delightful to be around little children is that they are so full of feeling. When they are happy to see you, they really feel their joy. When they love you, they really feel the love. As children, we all had the ability to feel at full capacity, but often as adults we lose that ability to various degrees. In coping with life's challenges and disappointments, we can become numb to our emotions. By not feeling anger, sadness, fear, and sorrow, we eventually lose our ability to feel love, joy, gratitude, and peace. By making sure that we do not suppress our negative emotions, we can keep our hearts open.

By not feeling our negative feelings, we gradually lose our ability to feel positive feelings.

Without understanding and experiencing how negative emotions can be released, we will always be concerned they will bring us down. Yet, once we learn how to feel all four healing emotions, we cannot only heal a broken heart, but also make sure that it grows back stronger than before. Although it may seem hard to imagine right now, after healing a broken heart, we are able to love and enjoy life even more fully than before.

A SCARY MOVIE

I remember when I first made the connection that feelings need to be balanced. About eighteen years ago, I was sitting in a movie theater waiting to see a scary movie. I usually don't like horror movies, but my friends told me this one was also very spiritual. Even though it was just a movie, I became very nervous and anxious. While sitting there, vague fears about horror movies started to come up.

My date and I were the only people in the theater. Right before the movie started, a really tall guy wearing a cowboy hat sat down right in front of me. He was so inconsiderate and rude to block my view in an empty theater. What a jerk, I thought. I was immediately furious. I didn't realize that he was oblivious that he was blocking my view. He was so tall he had never experienced having his view blocked in a theater.

In those days I didn't possess the basic skill to ask him politely to move. Instead, I sat there getting angrier and angrier. After about three or four minutes, I decided to go for revenge. I got up and sat down right in front of him with my date. Eventually I realized that he could not care less. He had not even noticed what had happened.

As I sat there feeling angry and a little relieved that I had done something, I realized that all my nervousness and anxiety about the movie had disappeared. As we continued to wait for the movie to start, I realized I was no longer nervous. Somehow, when I got angry, my anxiety went away.

I reasoned that my tendency to suppress anger unless really provoked had somehow caused me to be more fearful. As a result of denying my feelings of anger, my fears had become stronger. To test this out, I developed and began practicing a little anger process every time I felt some anxiety. I begin to find immediate relief. By balancing my fears with the expression of anger, my anxiety went away.

NEW DISCOVERIES

From my own personal discovery, I began to explore how my clients were blocking various negative emotions in their lives. Some were stuck feeling angry because they could not cry. Others cried easily, but could not get angry. As a result they become stuck in their grief. Fear and insecurity paralyzed others, because they had not taken enough time to feel their sadness or anger. Others were stuck in sorrow and unable to love, because they had not confronted their fears.

People were stuck in so many ways simply because their past conditioning prevented them from recognizing and feeling one or two of the four healing emotions. I discovered that every negative state was the direct result of an imbalance of negative emotions. With the correct balance, a healing release automatically took place. Negative feelings were automatically replaced by positive feelings of relief, peace, love, understanding, forgiveness, and trust.

All negative states are the direct result
of an imbalance of negative emotions.

This was a different way of looking at negative emotions. Prior to this realization, I thought negative emotions were the problem and not the solution. With this new insight, rather than encouraging my clients to try to get rid of negative emotions, or to try to express them, I suggested that my clients *expand* their awareness of negative emotions to include all four healing emotions. As a result, particularly when they felt stuck in an emotion, shifting to another emotion would in almost all cases provide *immediate* relief. After working with thousands of clients and workshop participants, I was eventually able to forge and refine this new understanding of the four healing emotions.

GETTING STUCK IN ANGER

If a person is not able to feel sadness, fear, or sorrow, then it is easy to get stuck feeling angry. Due to social conditioning, men particularly have trouble admitting to feelings of sadness, fear, and sorrow. It is more acceptable for a man to feel anger. This limitation causes men to pay a heavy price. When they finally experience the other negative emotions, they are overwhelmed. It is as though all the hurt of a lifetime comes up. Though this is very difficult to handle, if a man is able to complete the grieving process, he will be free once and for all of the conditioning that limits many men.

When either a man or a woman is unable to

acknowledge and share his or her fear and sorrow, the ability to give and receive love will be restricted. If a man experiences a broken heart but is unable to acknowledge his more vulnerable emotions, he may become overly demanding, defensive, or indifferent in subsequent relationships. As soon as he begins to feel increasing love and intimacy, his unresolved feelings of sadness, fear, and sorrow become activated.

To avoid having to deal with these unresolved feelings once again, his automatic tendency is to pull away. He will begin to feel powerless to get what he needs, become confused about his feelings, and question his commitment. Just as he suppressed these feelings before, he will do it again. Although he will feel justified, he will tend to become increasingly demanding, defensive, and indifferent.

GETTING STUCK IN VULNERABLE FEELINGS

In a similar way, when a person is not able to experience his or her feelings of anger, then it is easy to get stuck in emotions like sadness, fear, and sorrow. Women particularly have trouble admitting to feelings of anger. Society mistakenly frowns on women saying "no" or expressing anger. From the time they are little girls, women are taught to be desirable and not to desire. They are conditioned to be sweet and loving and not encouraged to set limits, or to show anger.

> From the time they are little girls,
> women are taught to be desirable
> and not to desire.

To heal a broken heart, a woman must be able to overcome this limitation in the expression of her feelings. The permission to be angry is essential if she is ever to trust love again. Without feeling the power and clarity that results from anger, her fears, grief, and sorrow can seem unlimited. After a broken heart, women commonly avoid getting involved again to avoid sinking into the darkness of these feelings.

Unless the vulnerable feelings are balanced with the expression of anger, just the thought of getting involved can bring up these unresolved painful feelings. To avoid this discomfort, a woman may avoid getting involved again. Unable to release her pain, if she has not felt and released her anger, she will tend to become depressed, mistrusting, and rigid. She becomes her biggest obstacle to finding love once again.

EMOTIONS ARE NOT GENDER BASED

Although women commonly have problems feeling and releasing angry, aggressive emotions and men commonly have difficulty experiencing their more vulnerable feelings, these differences are not innate. Our ability to feel our emotions is not a gender difference. Instead, the ability is greatly influenced by our parents, society, and early childhood experiences. Men and women equally need to feel the four healing emotions.

Our ability to feel our
emotions is not a gender difference.
Instead, this ability is greatly influenced
by our parents, society, and early
childhood experiences.

Although society's conditioning has caused men to suppress vulnerable feelings and women to suppress aggressive feelings, there are *many* exceptions, particularly when the heart is broken. If given the opportunity, men can feel just as vulnerable as women and women can be just as aggressive as men.

As a counselor, I have repeatedly witnessed that my clients, men or women, would begin to heal their hearts most effectively if equal attention was given to each of the four healing emotions. As a general rule, I found that the emotion that was easiest for the client to feel and talk about was masking other emotions. It was just the tip of the iceberg.

Progress can only be achieved by exploring the deeper levels beneath the surface of the mind. Quite often, a full release took place only after going back to examine other times in their past when a certain painful feeling was not fully experienced. Once all four healing emotions were expressed, they were free to experience the underlying positive feelings of love, understanding, for-giveness, and gratitude. Let's look at a few exam-ples.

STUCK IN SADNESS AND FEAR

Mary's husband Richard died of a heart attack at thirty-eight. Five years after his death, she came for counseling. She was depressed. She said that her life was empty without Richard. There was no joy. When I asked her about her grieving process she said it had taken years, but she really hadn't got over it. She was so sad. For months she had cried and cried without feeling much relief. For years, she couldn't even think of getting involved in another relationship. Her father had died when she was young, and it was just too much when her husband died. It was just too painful to love again. As a result, she resisted getting involved with a new man.

When we lose love, we may feel it is
too painful to love again.

Mary was eventually able to release her fears and sadness by giving herself permission to be angry. Prior to counseling, she would never have even considered getting angry. It just didn't seem loving at all. Mary had spent years feeling her sor-row, sadness, and fear, but never came out of it. By giving herself permission to explore, feel, and express her anger, she was gradually able to move on and find love again. She even expressed her anger with God for taking away her father. Experiencing her anger reconnected her with her passion for love and life and eventually fueled her courage to get involved again. Until she was able to acknowledge her anger, her fears held her back.

STUCK IN ANGER AND RESENTMENT

Tom felt good about his divorce. He was relieved to get out and be free. When he was married, he had been completely frustrated. He felt that no matter what he did for his wife it was never enough. No matter what he said, it was the wrong thing. He explained, "She was just too demanding. There was no fun. A relationship should be fun."

After his divorce, he started having fun again. It was such a relief to play his music, follow his schedule, eat what he wanted, and see the movies he wanted to see. He began dating again, had lots of fun, but when a relationship got serious, he would back off. To him, it seemed that every woman he met eventually became too demanding, just like his wife.

Although Tom was a positive guy and he wished his ex well, he was still angry when he talked about his partner. He resented that his efforts had not been appreciated. His way of coping with anger was simply to blame, move on, and make sure that he never got involved again with another demanding woman. Although he did not realize it, he was stuck in his anger, and it was affecting all his relationships. At a certain point in each new relationship, he would begin to feel his anger, blame his partner, and move on.

The way we cope with the loss of love
reveals how we may automatically cope
with love in the future.

Tom expected a mate to be light, cheerful, and always satisfied with him. He thought of himself as easygoing and wanted a partner who was the same. When a woman expressed a desire for more, he would react defensively. He would blame her for being too demanding. Tom had not realized that his expectations of a relationship were unrealistic. He could not see how he was the demanding one.

In counseling he began to understand how unrealistic his expectations were. He learned that it is normal for men and women to have different reactions to things and that a loving relationship requires accepting those differences. In his mind, he could eventually accept a woman's need to share negative feelings, but he would still be disturbed when his partner seemed upset. To adjust his expectations on an emotional level, he needed to heal his heart. Then we looked at how he had not fully grieved the failure of his marriage six years earlier.

To adjust expectations on an emotional
level we must heal the heart.

When he divorced, it never occurred to him to explore the four healing emotions. He was so relieved, he didn't realize there was a wound to be healed. As we talked about what had happened, he was able to feel some anger, but he didn't experience any sadness or sorrow. He was glad that the relationship was over.

Eventually, by focusing on how he felt in the beginning of the relationship, he was able to feel some sadness and disappointment. But clearly he was blocked. When I asked him to remember a time when he did feel disappointed, he remembered the loss of his father, which occurred when he was twelve years old.

His father had died in a car accident, which was devastating to his mother and to him. Someone at the funeral told him he had to be strong for his mother. He worked hard to hold back his tears and not to show his sorrow. He tried to be cheerful so that he wouldn't be a burden to his mother. By recalling that time and giving himself permission to feel all four healing emotions, he was gradually able to heal his heart, which had broken at that young and vulnerable age.

When a feeling is blocked
in our past, until it is unblocked
we will have difficulty fully feeling
that level of emotion.

In Tom's adult years, he couldn't tolerate sadness and disappointment from his partners, because these feelings were still unresolved within him. As long as he was not willing to feel his own sadness and grief, he could not tolerate disappointment in his relationships. He would react defensively with anger and blame.

By embracing his own feelings, he was gradually able to adjust his expectations and to understand his partner's need to feel upset at times. With this crucial adjustment, he was able to be less defensive and demanding of his partner.

STUCK IN SORROW AND SELF-PITY

Danna had been married twelve years. Her husband, Rex, had left her for his younger secretary. She had been single again for more than ten years. When she talked about Rex, she did so in a tone of self-pity and hopelessness. In her mind, he had basically ruined her life. Over the years, she had told her story many times, but was still unable to let go and move on. From her point of view, life would never be as good.

Danna was stuck in her feelings of sorrow. She couldn't let go and move on. As long as she held on to missing Rex, she was able to avoid facing her fears of being rejected again. Deep inside, she felt inadequate and unworthy of love. She was afraid that no one would ever love her. Until she could admit this fear, she could not release it.

This is the problem with negative emotions. Most of them are irrational. They are based on erroneous beliefs. To release these beliefs, we must first feel the negative emotions. To maintain her pride, she was unwilling to admit, even to herself, her fear that she was unworthy of ever finding love again.

To release erroneous beliefs we must first feel negative emotions.

In counseling, remembering the time when she was in love with Rex, she was able to begin to feel her sadness. She remembered how much she loved him and the special times they shared together. She remembered how much it hurt when he left. Staying with her sadness, she was then able to feel a little deeper. She discovered that a part of her was terrified that she would never find love again. She was afraid of trusting and being hurt again.

After she could feel the fear, we went further back in time. She was able to remember another time in her life when she was also afraid. She remembered her father yelling and being mean to her mother. Although he had not treated her that way, she was still afraid that he could. To avoid his anger, she would try to be really good. Deep inside, she believed that, if she freely expressed her feelings or did what she wanted, she would lose his love and be punished.

She had difficulty being angry with her father, because he wasn't that mean to her. What she didn't understand is that she could still be angry about the things he didn't do. She realized he didn't make it safe for her to be herself. He had not taken time to find out who she was, what she felt, and what she wanted and needed. This extra insight gave Danna a reason to be angry. By giving herself permission to be angry about his neglect, Danna was eventually able to release her fears.

OPENING UP TO LOVE AGAIN

Using this approach in thousands of cases, I have found that by fully feeling each of the four healing emotions, counseling clients and participants in Personal Success Workshops were able to release the pain of the past and open up to increasing love, abundance, and success in their lives. Quite often a person had already done more than enough grieving at two or three healing emotions, but until they were able to grieve at the missing level they were not able to move on successfully.

In most cases, when we are blocked at a particular level, it is extremely helpful to recall events in our past when that particular feeling was not fully acknowledged, shared, or allowed. If you know what you are looking for, it can generally be found very easily. By asking the right question, the missing feeling automatically comes up.

To open our hearts, as in each of the above examples, we must be careful to counteract our past personal conditioning and experience each of the four healing emotions fully. Besides our past conditioning, there are other ways we block feeling a particular healing emotion. In the next chapter we will explore how loss can prevent us from feeling all four healing emotions. With this added insight, we can then focus our attention on bringing up the missing emotions in order to complete the healing with love, acceptance, understanding, and trust.

6

GOOD ENDINGS MAKE GOOD BEGINNINGS

No one falls in love thinking, "Let's get together and then, after a few happy years' experience, have a painful breakup." When we fall in love, we don't plan to lose that love. In the beginning, love always feels as if it's forever, but we can lose it. When it happens, it breaks our hearts.

The end of an intimate relationship is a devastating loss regardless of the conditions leading up to it. How we grieve that loss will determine the rest of lives. Whether a relationship ends by death, divorce, or other circumstances, we must take special care to complete the grieving process. Good endings make good beginnings.

Regardless of how a relationship ends, we must take special care to complete the grieving process.

To move on in our lives and to find love again, we must fully feel and grieve our loss. Yet different circumstances surrounding the end of a relationship can make the healing process confusing and difficult. Without clear insight into what is required of us, we may unknowingly sabotage the natural healing process in a variety of ways.

GRIEVING A TRAGEDY

As I have described in my introduction, while on my honeymoon, I received a call that my father had died. I was stunned, enraged, and horrified all at the same time. I cried out, "How could this happen? Who would do such a thing? It's not right. It's unfair. Why would anybody do this?"

Although I had helped many others through their tragedies, I had not yet experienced such a devastating loss personally. With the support of family and friends, along with a few workshops, I was fully able to experience and to complete the healing process. Although in the beginning, I felt I would always be in pain, the pain was healed with time. When the pain left, my heart was filled with acceptance and love. I could never have anticipated or imagined how much I grew from this experience.

When the pain in our hearts is
healed, we are left with loving
memories and peace.

As I explained earlier, my father had picked up a hitchhiker, who robbed him and then left him in the trunk. After lying in the trunk for several hours, he eventually died of heatstroke. After the funeral, I wanted to connect with my father and in some way share his experience. Some part of me really wanted to feel what he might have gone through. With my mother and siblings around me, I got into the trunk and they closed the lid.

As I lay inside the trunk, which was not as confining as I had imagined, I saw the marks where he had banged on the roof with a screwdriver. Hoping someone would hear his call and rescue him, he had continued to pound. I saw where he had tried to pry open the latch. Then I discovered he had pulled back one of the rear light encasements to get air.

Automatically, I extended my hand through the hole for a brief moment. As I was pulling my hand back in, my brother on the outside said, "See if you can reach around and push the button." I stretched my arm out the hole, reached over, and pushed the button, and the trunk opened.

We were stunned. If he only had thought of this, he would still be alive. When trying to get out of a trunk, one doesn't think about how one could get in. I certainly didn't think of it. It took my brother on the outside to notice the button. Without that one insight, my father remained trapped until he died.

Over the months that followed his death, I continued to process my anger about the robbery and mistreatment of my father, and I felt my sadness that my father was no longer in my life. I faced my own fears of dying locked in that trunk and felt my sorrow that I could not do anything to bring back my dad or to prevent his suffering. Listening to and talking with others who had suffered similar losses eventually made the process less difficult. Although it brought up the pain, it was also helping to heal the pain.

Unless we can feel our pain,
we cannot heal it.

Gradually, instead of feeling an agonizing knot in my heart, remembering my father got easier. Although I didn't like talking about what had happened, I knew it was an essential part of the healing process. After much sharing, I began to feel the warmth of my father's love for me and the sweetness of my love for him. This was an important shift. After any loss, when we can think back and feel our love without pain then the healing process is complete. Still, to this day, when I think about my father and his tragic death, a wonderful feeling of love and peace comes over me.

When we can think back and
feel our love without pain,
the healing process is complete.

I feel I was lucky to have this understanding of how to grieve a loss. There are hundreds of thousands of people who don't move on after a tragic loss. Instead of finding peace, they quietly suffer their loss for years. Unaware that there is a way to heal their broken hearts, they remain stuck.

LOSING A SPOUSE

When we lose a loved one in a tragic accident, it is important to know that our grief is not supposed to be permanent. Without an understanding of how we can heal pain, we confuse our grief with the fact that we love the person we have lost.

We mistakenly believe that if we truly loved someone, then we will always feel the pain of losing them.

Without this understanding, the thought of feeling better, feeling good, or even feeling really happy seems to minimize our genuine feelings of loss. To be happy again implies that we have forgotten a loved one. With the loss of a spouse, we may even feel it would be a betrayal if we were to love again. This kind of thinking can greatly obstruct the natural healing process, preventing us from ever letting go.

If we believe in our mind that it is "not loving" to let go of our sadness then we will continue to hold on to it in our hearts. Just as the mind can suppress negative feelings, it can also keep us from letting go by suppressing positive feelings.

> To fully heal our hearts, we must not
> only feel our negative emotions, but
> also give ourselves permission to let go
> and feel happy again.

Eventually, as the heart heals, when we think about our loss, we may still feel some sadness and miss our partners, but the dominant feeling becomes the warmth of our love for them. Instead of causing pain, remembering the special times we shared brings up feelings of peace and gratitude. Instead of feeling empty and alone, we feel love surrounding and supporting us as we begin to rebuild our lives.

Although some may believe unending grief to be the symptom of a deep and real love, it is not. Certainly, the love is real, but the despair is the result of not completing the grieving process. Unending sorrow is not a testament to our undying love, but rather a sickness that requires a cure. No one is meant to live a life without love. More tragic than any death is continuing to live with a broken heart. To love again does not mean that we have stopped loving those whom we lost.

> More tragic than any death is
> continuing to live with a broken heart.

Even with this insight we may still remain stuck. If we continue to look for the missing level of emotion whenever we are stuck, we can eventually find it. Unless we know what to look for, we could easily spend the rest of our lives stuck in grief. This is why it is crucial that we understand fully how to feel each of the four levels. It is not enough simply to experience whatever we feel. In most cases, we have to search our souls to find the missing levels of emotion.

To heal our hearts, it is not enough
simply to feel whatever we feel.

When we have lived our lives suppressing particular feelings in certain kinds of circumstances, it is not easy to find them. Past conditioning prevents us from freely feeling each of the four healing emotions. Private counseling sessions, workshops, support groups, and self-help exercises are essential because they create opportunities to break free from our past conditioning and to feel our hidden emotions.

THE POWER TO HEAL OUR HEARTS

Although we already have the power to heal ourselves, we still need others to assist us in the healing process. If you are a doctor with a broken bone, even though you know what needs to be done, you would still go to another expert for their assistance. In a similar way, when our hearts are broken, we need to seek out skilled assistance and caring support. We cannot do it alone.

In a workshop or support group, our hidden feelings can be easily discovered. Suppressed feelings automatically come up simply because someone else is sharing that feeling. On your own, you would never feel that emotion, but sitting in the workshop, the release automatically takes place.

Buried feelings automatically come up when someone else shares the same emotion we are suppressing.

For example, when someone else who is not blocked at the level of anger shares, the part of you that is angry wakes up. Even if your conditioning dictates that you not feel anger, a sleeping part of you awakens and you become unstuck, just as at the end of a good tearjerker movie tears of release automatically stream down and you find relief. These are not the tears of despair or self-pity that leave you feeling low. These tears make you feel better.

Healing tears do not leave you feeling low. They make you feel better.

Workshops and support groups help us to get in touch with feelings. A sustained relationship with a counselor can create the safety and trust to go deeper into our feelings. By sharing ourselves with someone who understands loss, we feel safe enough to explore deeper levels of feeling. When a counselor is trained to ask the right questions at the right time, then the hidden feelings come up and we find release.

Self-help exercises are also very effective, but their effectiveness dramatically increases when used in conjunction with private therapy, workshops, and support groups. All of the exercises suggested throughout this book can be done alone, but can also be done with the assistance of a counselor or support group. Exploring wounded feelings in the presence of others, particularly in the early stages of healing an emotional wound, is the ideal. Our own pain becomes more bearable to the extent that someone else can relate to it. When we share our pain, it is released and healed more effectively.

THE CHALLENGES OF HEALING

Every circumstance of loss has its own unique challenges. Carol lost her husband Steve in a sudden and tragic car accident. She had warned him to use a seat belt. After receiving the news of his death, she found out that he had not heeded her warning and, instead of being injured, he died. After his death, she also discovered that they had huge financial problems which now had become her burden.

One part of her felt sad, but another part was angry and afraid. This was very confusing. Most people are not used to feeling more than one emotion at the same time. In this case, Carol felt sad because she loved and missed Steve, but she also felt angry because Steve hadn't used his seat belt. In addition, she was afraid of her new financial burden. Without understanding the importance of taking time to experience and explore each level of her emotions, she became overwhelmed and stuck.

At the funeral, she felt sadness, but some secret part of her, deep inside, was also holding on to anger and blame. It seemed unloving to have feelings of anger, so she kept pushing them down. Yet she was angry. She blamed Steve for not heeding her warning and for leaving her with so many burdens. The fear she felt regarding her new responsibilities fueled more anger and blame.

As Carol continued to push down her feelings of anger, feeling genuine sadness became difficult. As long as she was pushing down the anger and fear, she was unable to feel fully and release her sadness. The sadness she did feel was transformed into self-pity. She was even able to cry, but her tears did not bring relief. She was left feeling an aching numbness in her heart.

When our anger is suppressed, our
sadness turns to self-pity.

In this example, we can see how the grieving process becomes much more complicated. We miss our partner, but we also blame and resent him or her. Instead of giving ourselves permission to be angry, we block our feelings by thinking we should just be sad. Since we do not want to be a burden to others or cause others to think negatively about our deceased spouse, we do not share our fears. We hold it all in, trying to be strong.

Without being able to share our many feelings in confidence with another, the blame we feel may follow us wherever we go. We may feel like a victim for the rest of our lives. Since we walk around feeling "unloving" thoughts of anger and blame, we may also begin to feel the increased weight of guilt. We feel bad because we are not loving our partner as we used to. No matter how much we try to find our tender feelings of love, we end up feeling annoyed or completely numb.

In counseling, Carol was finally able to disclose her hidden feelings of anger and fear. She was then able to feel and release her sadness and sorrow. Her guilt went away, and she began to feel much better about herself and more hopeful that she could handle her new responsibilities.

GETTING STUCK IN ANGER

Sharron and Ed argued all the time. Their values were just too different for them to get along. After they separated, Sharron felt a range of feelings. Her dominant feeling was anger, but fueling her anger was fear. She was afraid that her nine-year-old son, Nathan, was being parented incorrectly when he spent time with his dad. She thought he was spoiling Nathan.

Sharron was teaching him the importance of earning money, while Ed would freely buy him whatever he wanted. She wanted Nathan to do chores, and his father would say yes to whatever Nathan wanted. She felt sorry that she was powerless to protect him from this confusion.

Sharron's fear and sorrow about Nathan actually fueled her anger toward Ed. Instead of letting go of her anger about the separation, she became even more angry. As the months passed, Nathan began to experience new problems at school, which made Sharron feel even angrier.

To make matters worse, she had less time to be there for her son. To support herself after the separation, she had to go back to work. She felt sad that Nathan was not finishing his school projects, but it was hard for her to give him the compassion and understanding he needed. Each day she was feeling guilty and angry. She felt guilty that she couldn't spend more time with him and angry with Ed.

**It is hard to be compassionate
when we are angry.**

Sharron had never taken enough time to grieve the ending of her marriage. As a result, the frustrations of parenting weighed much more heavily on her soul. When our hearts are not healed, we become overly sensitive to the problems of living. Often it feels like someone is poking at an open wound. She was so angry she wasn't able to cope with her son's problems. When she was short or insensitive with him, she felt even more guilt. This then fueled more anger toward Ed.

As you can see, matters were getting worse. At a Mars-Venus workshop, however, Sharron learned about the four healing emotions. She realized that she hadn't really grieved and healed the end of her marriage. She had felt anger but not sadness. By taking time to feel her sadness and grieve her loss, she was eventually able to forgive Ed and to realize that it wasn't all his fault. He really wasn't the right man for her.

By taking time to feel our sadness,
we are eventually able to let go of
our anger and to forgive.

As she cried tears of sadness, her anger softened and she was able to feel some love and appreciation for Ed. Remembering the love they had shared in the beginning helped her to let go with love. She could feel grateful for the good times and also feel good about herself. It released her from feeling so foolish about getting married in the first place. As a result, she felt more confident that she could find a lasting relationship in the future.

Sharron recognized the importance to saying good things about Ed in front of Nathan. She also realized that the qualities she resisted in Ed were also in Nathan. By learning to accept and to see the good in Ed, it made it easier for Nathan to deal with the difference between his parents. Sharron learned that she could disagree with Ed's values without putting him down.

When a young boy hears good things about his

father, he can feel good about the parts of him that are like his dad. Sharron was motivated to forgive Ed not just because it was good for her but for the sake of her son as well.

There is no greater gift parents can give their children than to love each other.

As Sharron gave herself permission to dig deeper and explore her feelings of sadness, she was able to release her angry feelings and feel more loving. Not only was she happier, but her son was happier as well. This kind of "good ending" made Sharron more receptive to getting involved again. Sharron eventually remarried the right man for her and had more children.

HOLDING BACK OUR FEELINGS

When we hold back our feelings because they don't seem loving, it is time to seek help. While it may not feel safe to share our feelings of anger with our family and friends, we can safely share them with a therapist. This is the best time to talk with a counselor, to take a healing workshop, or to join a support group.

Often we hold back our anger because we are afraid it is not loving.

To find relief, it is our responsibility to create an appropriate setting to share our nonloving feelings in a context where no one gets hurt, or we are not judged as being too negative. Once we are free to explore and share all our feelings, our hearts can begin to heal, gradually opening up to feelings of forgiveness, understanding, love, and trust.

A skilled counselor will not judge what we feel, but by listening and asking questions will draw out the various emotions that need to be felt and expressed. To share feelings without being concerned that it will hurt someone, or that it will be used against us, frees our heart to heal itself. Creating this safety to share all our feelings is like putting the cast on a broken arm to protect it while the healing occurs.

By sharing the complete truth about our feelings, we are ensuring that we will find love again. No matter what the circumstances, with the correct approach, we can release our pain and open the door to find love. By working to create a good ending, we are assured of creating a good beginning. When our hearts are open, we are most capable of finding the love we want, need, and deserve.

7

THE FEELING BETTER EXERCISE

Remembering and grieving for our partner should leave us feeling better, but sometimes just getting in touch with our feelings doesn't complete the healing process. We may feel our pain, but we don't find relief. This is generally because we are overlooking some important part of the process and are thereby limiting our natural ability to heal. One of the best ways to exercise and strengthen our ability to heal our hearts is to practice the feeling better exercise. By practicing this technique, you will become adept at being able to heal any hurt.

One of the best ways to exercise our ability to heal is to practice the feeling better exercise.

Although there are hundreds of ways and processes to get in touch with our painful feelings, unless we know the fundamentals of healing pain, we may not be successful in letting go and finding love again. Practicing the feeling better excrcise trains us in the process of making sure we are able to heal the hurt we get in touch with. If we cannot heal a hurt, then we may remain stuck in our pain and gradually suppress it.

WRITING A FEELING LETTER

When you are feeling an emotional pain, then take about twenty minutes to write out your feelings in this particular manner. In the beginning, it is best to write out or type your feelings. After you have become more skilled at this process, you can do it by sitting with eyes closed or by sharing with a counselor or group.

I have been practicing this particular exercise for seventeen years, and sometimes I still benefit most by writing out my feelings. When something really bothers me, I will sit down in front of the computer and directly type out my feelings following the basic format of the feeling better exercise.

The feeling better exercise has three parts:

1. Expressing the four healing emotions along with our wants, needs, and wishes

2. Expressing the loving and understanding response that we would like to hear

3. Expressing forgiveness, understanding, gratitude, and trust

Let's explore each part in greater detail.

PART ONE: EXPRESSING OUR FEELINGS

The first part of the feeling better exercise is to write a letter to the person whom you are upset about losing. You can also write a feeling letter to someone you can imagine really hearing you—a good friend or an angel from God. Make sure that you explore each of the four healing emotions. If you want to change the order, that is fine. Start with the feelings that you feel most strongly. Take about two or three minutes to feel each of the four healing emotions.

While writing the letter, imagine that the person is hearing everything you say. Imagine that he is able to hear your feelings and then will be able to respond with understanding and support. Even if in real life the person could not hear your feelings, for the purpose of healing your heart, imagine how you would feel and what you would say if he could hear your feelings.

THE FEELING LETTER FORMAT

Dear _____ ,

I am writing this letter to share my pain in order to find acceptance, forgiveness, and love.

Right now, I . . .

1. *I feel angry that . . .*
   I feel angry because . . .
   I feel angry when . . .
   I don't like . . .
   I wish . . .

2. *I feel sad that . . .*
   I feel sad because . . .
   I feel sad when . . .
   I wanted . . .
   I expect . . .

3. *I feel afraid that . . .*
   I feel afraid because . . .
   I feel afraid when . . .
   I do not want . . .
   I need . . .

4. *I feel sorry that . . .*
   I feel sorry because . . .
   I feel sorry when . . .
   I want . . .
   I hope . . .

   Thank you for listening.

   Love, _____

PART TWO: EXPRESSING A SUPPORTIVE RESPONSE

To take responsibility to heal our pain instead of depending on some outside source for love and support, we must learn to give it to ourselves. This ability is very easy. Just as we would be supportive of someone else in pain, we give ourselves the support we need. After first writing out our feelings, the next step is creating and expressing a loving response. Just as we need to put our feelings into words, it is very important to put into words the support we need to feel nurtured, understood, and supported.

In part two, we write a letter to ourselves. We pretend that we are the person with whom we are sharing and write the response we would want to hear. If you are imagining that you are sharing your feelings with a friend or an angel from God, then write out what you feel she would say to you. Say whatever makes you feel heard and nurtured. To help create a response, you may benefit by using this response letter format.

THE RESPONSE LETTER FORMAT

Dear _____,

1. *Thank you for . . .*
2. *I understand . . .*
3. *I am sorry . . .*
4. *Please forgive me for . . .*
5. *I want you to know . . .*
6. *You deserve . . .*
7. *I want . . .*

Sometimes writing the response letter is more powerful than writing out the four healing emotions. Writing out what we actually want and need to hear increases our openness to receiving the support we deserve. By imagining this support, we are opening our hearts once more to heal our pain.

PART THREE: EXPRESSING POSITIVE FEELINGS

After we have written out the response that would make us feel most supported, then it is important to express and affirm our positive feelings of forgiveness, understanding, gratitude, and trust.

To assist you in writing out your positive feelings, you may wish to follow this completion letter format.

THE COMPLETION LETTER FORMAT

1. *Thank you for . . .*
2. *I understand . . .*
3. *I realize that . . .*
4. *I know . . .*
5. *I forgive . . .*
6. *I am grateful for . . .*
7. *I trust that . . .*
8. *Right now in my life I am in the process of . . .*

By taking the time to affirm your positive feelings, you will feel much better. Sometimes in the beginning, after doing this process you will feel a little drained. As you improve, the exercise will leave you refreshed.

A SAMPLE FEELING LETTER

The following is an example of how Bill used the feeling better exercise to get in touch with the four healing emotions of his feelings. He simply used each of the lead-in phrases to draw out a particular feeling. As you practice this technique, feel free to repeat a particular lead-in phrase as many times as you would like before moving on to the next one. If you wish to skip one, that is fine, too. Use the format as a tool to assist you in getting in touch with and giving expression to the four healing emotions within you.

Dear Susan,

I am writing this letter to share my pain in order to find acceptance, forgiveness, and love.

Right now I am feeling alone, hurt, abandoned, and betrayed.

1. *I feel angry that you left.*
   I feel angry because you feel in love with someone else.
   I feel angry when I think about the two of you together.
   I don't like being rejected.
   I wish you still loved me.
2. *I feel sad that you are not in my life.*
   I feel sad because I don't know where to turn.
   I feel sad when I think about how much I love you.
   I wanted to live happily ever after; I wanted you to love me.
   I expected you to love me and keep your promise.
3. *I feel afraid that I was a fool.*
   I feel afraid because I don't know what I did wrong.

I feel afraid when I think about starting over.
I do not want to be alone.
I need your love and friendship.
4. *I feel sorry that we are not together.*
   I feel sorry because I can't change your mind.
   I feel sorry when I think about the love we
   shared.
   I want you to love me. I want to be married.
   I hope I can learn to let go.
   Thank you for listening.

Love, Bill

A SAMPLE RESPONSE LETTER

Dear Bill,

1. *Thank you for sharing your feelings with me.*
2. *I understand how much I have hurt your feelings.*
3. *I am sorry, I am so sorry that I don't love you anymore the way I did, I am sorry things have changed.*
4. *Please forgive me for leaving you and rejecting you.*
5. *I want you to know that I love you but you are not the right person for me. I will always cherish our time together. I am so grateful for your love and support.*
6. *You deserve to be loved by someone and have a great relationship.*

7. *I want you to be happy. I want you to find love again.*

Love, Susan

A SAMPLE COMPLETION LETTER

Dear Susan,

1. *Thank you for loving me. I will always love you.*
2. *I understand that I have to let go, and I will eventually.*
3. *I realize that these things take time. I feel very hurt and it will take time to heal.*
4. *I know you love me in your own way. I know I do not own you and you are free to do as you want.*
5. *I forgive you for not loving me. I forgive you for leaving me. I forgive you for not giving me a chance.*
6. *I am grateful for the many years we did spend together.*
7. *I trust that I will find love again and I will get over this.*
8. *Right now in my life I am in the process of starting over and rebuilding my life. I am doing what I need to find love and happiness again. I know things will get better.*

Love, Bill

THE FOUR QUESTIONS

Another way to process the four healing emotions is simply to ask yourself these four questions. Often men find this an easier approach in the beginning. By answering these questions, our healing emotions automatically begin to come up. While answering these questions, give yourself permission to feel anger, sadness, fear, sorrow, and any other similar feelings.

1. What happened?

2. What didn't happen?

3. What could happen?

4. What can't happen?

If you wish to explore a little deeper, there are a few more questions you can ask and answer.

THE FOUR QUESTIONS

QUESTION ONE

> **What happened** that you didn't want to
>   happen?
> What is happening that you don't want to
>   happen?
> What has happened that you do not like?

QUESTION TWO

What didn't happen that you wanted to
   happen?
What is not happening that you want to
   happen?
What should have happened?

QUESTION THREE

What could happen that you don't want to
   happen?
What is important to you?
What could happen that you want to happen?

QUESTION FOUR

What can't happen that you want to happen?
What can't happen that you wish could have
   happened?
What can happen that you want to happen?

By asking these four questions or practicing the
three parts of the feeling better exercise, you will
be better prepared to heal the waves of feeling that
come from your loss. With this technique, you will
be able to remember your partner without having
to get stuck in painful feelings. With this insight
and ability, you are free to stay in touch with your
feelings and complete the healing process.

8

FINDING FORGIVENESS

When we blame our partner for our unhappiness, we unknowingly prevent the release of painful feelings. Making our partner fully responsible for our pain causes us to hold on to our pain until she changes. This tendency is too limiting. As long as we make her fully responsible for our pain, we cannot release it. By blaming our partner for how we feel, we cannot let go of our hurt unless he corrects his behavior or attitude.

By blaming our partner for how
we feel, we cannot let go of
our hurt unless he corrects
his behavior or attitude.

Blame can be useful in healing our hearts, but then we need to release. Blame can help us set the boundaries of what we like and don't like. It also assists us in finding our anger and prevents us from taking on too much responsibility for a loss. Whenever we blame ourselves too much, it is because we do not give ourselves permission to blame others.

Once we have used blame to get in touch with our anger, we should then work on releasing it. Certainly others are to blame for their mistakes, but they are not to blame for our feelings. To forgive is to release another from being responsible for how we feel. By finding forgiveness, we are then free to let go of our pain.

To forgive is to release another from being responsible for how we feel.

Although it is true that our partner may make us feel upset, we must also recognize that we have the power to let go of our pain. When we blame him for our pain rather than for his mistakes, we become caught in our pain. When we are angry or sad that he neglected us, these feelings will pass. When we are angry or sad that we have been hurt, then we become stuck. When we feel powerless to change our feelings, then we begin to blame our partner for how we feel instead of for what she did or did not do.

These are some examples of the difference between feeling statements and blaming statements. Take some time to imagine saying these phrases and feel the difference. Feeling statements connect us to our passion, while blaming statements leave us feeling stuck. Feeling statements empower us, while blaming statements make us feel like victims.

Feeling Statements	Blaming Statements
I feel angry that you don't treat me in a respectful way.	I feel angry that you make me so unhappy.
I feel angry and hurt that you would treat me this way.	I am angry that you would hurt me this way.
I am angry that you do get what you want and I don't.	I am angry because you make me feel so jealous.
I am angry that you were so late and you didn't even call.	I am angry that you scared me. I didn't know what to do.
I am hurt that you ignored me, you make others more important than me.	I am hurt that you make me feel ignored and so unimportant.
I am sad that you didn't get me a present.	I am sad that you make me feel unloved.
I am afraid that you will judge me.	I am afraid that you will make me feel bad.
I am angry that you were critical of me, or I am afraid you will be critical of me.	I am angry that you ruined my day, or I am afraid that you will ruin my day.
I am angry that you kept me waiting.	I am angry that you make me so angry.
I am afraid to talk with you.	I am afraid that you will upset me.

I am afraid you are not interested in what I have to say.	I am afraid you will make me feel really bad and uninteresting.
I am upset because you were rude to me.	I am upset because you make me so unhappy.
I am upset because you jerk me around. One minute you are loving and the next you are distant.	I am upset because you upset me so much.

It is okay to acknowledge how we feel in response to what our partner says and does. If our partner upsets us, it is important to acknowledge our feelings, but then we need to let go. When we go on to blame our partners for how we feel, we bring down not only them but ourselves as well. Making her responsible for how we continue to feel after an offense prevents us from letting go. As long as we blame another, we will stay upset until he is willing to change.

THE IMPORTANCE OF FORGIVENESS

This, in a nutshell, is why forgiveness is so important: Forgiveness frees us from continuing to hold on to our pain. It frees us to let go of our hurt. It frees us to feel better and to find love again. Feeling our emotions and then finding forgiveness makes us more capable of finding solutions to a problem.

When we explore our feelings with the intention to forgive, then we are less inclined to blame our partners. Even if we start out blaming our partners, by continuing to explore the four healing emotions with someone we are not blaming or by writing out our feelings, we can eventually release the blame.

When we share our feelings directly with the person we are blaming, then our tendency to express ourselves in blaming statements rather than feeling statements increases. It is not wrong to share our feelings with our partner, but we should pick a time when he is willing to listen, and also when we have already experienced, to a degree, a sense of forgiveness.

When we share our feelings first with someone we are not blaming, we can get to forgiveness much more easily.

To base our willingness to forgive on another's response is a losing proposition. It just affirms that we are blaming someone else for our pain, rather than for what she did or didn't do. When a partner is not having to defend herself against being responsible for how we feel, then she is able to hear us and respond in a much more favorable way.

Most books on communication wisely stress the importance of using "I feel" statements instead of "you" statements. Although this is true, we must also be careful that our "I" statements are not also blame statements. "I feel" statements can be just as blaming as "you" statements. In the name of using "I feel" statements, we can unknowingly push our partner away.

"I feel" statements can be just as
blaming as "you" statements.

If we take the time to experience our feelings and find forgiveness, our tendency to blame others for how we feel will be lessened. By learning to express our feelings without using blame statements, our partner will be much more receptive. By first finding forgiveness before sharing our feelings, needs, wants, and wishes, we will not be coming from a place of blame.

SHARING OUR FEELINGS WITHOUT BLAME

Women particularly are more motivated to share their feelings. Instinctively, a woman senses that by sharing her pain with someone who loves her, he will become motivated to do whatever he can to protect her and support her in the future. Sharing our pain can motivate others to support us.

Unless others know how we feel, they
cannot correct certain behaviors or
know what kind of support we need.

How we share our feelings determines whether someone can hear us. Women commonly use blaming statements to express their feelings. Instead of hearing their pain and being motivated to do something, men become defensive. Instead of feeling motivated, they may become even more resistant to change.

PUTTING OUR LIVES BACK TOGETHER

When we end a relationship and there are children involved, we must recognize that the relationship is not really over. We cannot end it, but we can change it. Although we are no longer married partners, we are parents and we will need to communicate in such a way that our ex-partner and co-parent does not feel blamed.

To put our lives back together, not only do we need to stop feeling like a victim, but we need to make sure that we don't communicate like one as well. Most of the problems between divorced co-parents come from communicating with blame statements, rather than cooling off or centering ourselves before sharing.

Although men and women argue and fight about finances, responsibilities, keeping promises, different values, disciplining the children, and scheduling time with their children, the real reason they fight is that they have not learned an alternative to blame statements. After a few minutes of an argument, we begin to argue about the way we are arguing.

When we are able to communicate our differences without a blaming attitude, our partners can hear our point of view. When both sides feel heard and respected and not blamed, then creative solutions can be found to resolve our differences and solve our problems.

Even if we use the wrong words, if our attitudes reflect that we have forgiven our partner, they will be able to hear our feelings and be moved in some positive manner. Without a knowledge of communication skills, we tend to blame the listener for becoming defensive rather than recognizing how we are communicating blame.

By recognizing and using our power to change our feelings, we are freed from blaming our partners for how we feel. Unless we are clear that we hold the power to release and transform our negative feelings, we will blame them for how we feel. We will hold on to our feelings of hurt and grow in resentment. In the next chapter we will explore other challenges we face, while giving ourselves the time and nurturing we need to complete the healing process.

9

SAYING GOOD-BYE WITH LOVE

At the end of a relationship there are only two directions we can go. We either grow in our ability to love, or we begin a gradual decline. Our challenge in starting over is to release our pain with forgiveness, understanding, gratitude, and trust. Saying good-bye in this way eventually leaves us feeling good about ourselves, our future, and our past. Although this is easy to say, it is more difficult to put into practice.

Without a complete understanding of what is required during the healing process, it is easy to get stuck in a variety of undesirable emotional states. It is not uncommon to be gripped by resentment, blame, indifference, guilt, insecurity, hopelessness, or jealousy and envy. These seven attitudes prevent us from fully loving again. They are clear indications that we are in need of healing. When they persist, it is a sign that we are neglecting a part of the healing process.

These seven attitudes are the opposite of the

four healing emotions. With these seven attitudes, neither feeling them nor resisting them will help. The more we feel them, the more painful they become. They are like emotional quicksand: The more we resist them, the more they pull us down.

The seven negative attitudes are
emotional quicksand: The more we
resist them, the more they pull us down.

Each of these negative states conveys a particular message. If we can hear the message, the messenger will go away. If we do not understand their message, they will keep knocking at our door. Only when the messenger is heard will he go away. The more we ignore him, the louder he will knock.

Each of the seven negative attitudes is a flashing neon sign pointing us in the direction of the pain we are ignoring. When the particular circumstances of our loss prevent us from fully feeling our pain, these negative attitudes arrive to point out what we are missing in the healing process. Each of these attitudes serves the purpose of revealing where in our hearts we are suppressing particular healing feelings and desires. When we are able to locate and heal our hidden pain, then these negative attitudes automatically disappear.

Each of the seven negative attitudes is a
flashing neon sign pointing us in the
direction of the pain we are ignoring.

The only way to be free from the grip of the seven negative attitudes is to heed their message.

1. LETTING GO OF RESENTMENT

The most common of the seven attitudes is resentment, particularly when the marriage or relationship that has ended was not loving or nurturing. We resent that we wasted our time. We resent that our hopes and expectations were not met. Although we gave of ourselves, we did not get back what we needed. No matter how hard we tried, our efforts were never enough for our partner. Though this resentment is certainly appropriate, it is a clear indicator that we are not yet ready to get involved again.

When we feel resentful, our biggest challenge is to say good-bye with forgiveness and love. Although we have a right to feel resentful, our new challenge is to remember the love we once felt and then forgive our ex-partner for his mistakes. By taking the time to grieve our loss fully, it is eventually possible to release all our resentments and to wish our partner well.

It is eventually possible to release
all our resentments and wish
our partner well.

To uncover our buried love, each of the four healing emotions may first need to be explored.

1. We may need to feel the anger that they wasted so much of our lives, betrayed us, or deprived us of the love and support that we deserved.

2. We may need to feel the sadness that the relationship is over, that we don't have someone to love, that it didn't work out.

3. We may need to feel the fear that we are fools or that we will be fooled again, that we don't know how to make a relationship work.

4. We may need to feel the sorrow that we cannot go back and make it work, that we cannot make up for lost time, that we cannot change our partner's feelings.

Then expressing our feelings of forgiveness and understanding will enable us to remember the love we shared in the beginning. Remembering the love is very important. Forgiveness is not real until we can remember our positive feelings of love for another.

THE MEANING OF FORGIVENESS

Sometimes we are unable to forgive because we really do not understand what it means to forgive. We sense that if we forgave our partners and felt love for them, we would have to return to the relationship. This is not true. The best way to say good-bye is with love. We love him, but he is not right for us. If we have to say "I don't love you anymore" in order to leave a relationship, then we will leave with a closed heart. It is hard to attract love in our lives when our hearts are closed.

To forgive our ex-partner does
not mean we have to return
to the relationship.

On the other hand, when our hearts are open, we are able to recognize more clearly the right person for us. We are most attracted to and will attract partners who have a potential to fulfill us instead of disappointing us. The ability to pick the right person comes from an open heart. If our heart is closed to one person, then it cannot be fully open to another. If thinking about our past closes our hearts, then it is much more difficult to find the love we seek in the future. Sometimes we may find a loving partner, but we are not able to appreciate what we have.

2. LETTING GO OF BLAME

Quite often, after ending a relationship, we will simply blame our ex-partner for the problems, feel a huge relief to get out, and then move on. We feel relieved because finally we are out, and we have another chance to find love and happiness. Although this reaction is certainly appropriate, it is a clear indicator that we are denying a host of unresolved feelings. If we continue to ignore these feelings and just move on, we will tend to attract partners who are perfect to trigger our unresolved feelings.

Feeling relief is a clear indicator
that we are denying a host of
unresolved feelings.

Men and women commonly feel relief for different reasons. A man feels relief when he blames his partner for their problems, while a woman feels relief that she doesn't have to feel responsible for the relationship anymore. Although we both feel relief, we need to look a little deeper to heal our hearts and to find the right partner next time.

A man is eager to forget what has happened, but he has not yet forgiven. His immediate solution to the failure of his relationship is to find another partner. Although he may have a positive attitude, when similar issues arise in future relationships, he will be quick to blame and will have a more difficult time finding forgiveness.

To find forgiveness, a man needs to explore how he contributed to the problems in the relationship. The more responsible a man feels, the more he is able to forgive. A forgiving and responsible attitude frees him from being too picky or reacting with blame in future relationships.

> To find forgiveness, a man needs to
> explore how he contributed to the
> problems in the relationship.

When a woman feels relief it is associated with an attitude of responsibility. Her relief comes from not having to feel responsible anymore to make a relationship work. She feels she has sacrificed enough and often has nothing left to give. In this state of mind, she must be careful not to be forgiving right away, otherwise she may get stuck in self-blame. When a relationship fails, men get most stuck by blaming their partner while women get most stuck by blaming themselves.

To forgive and forget, women need first to explore how they were affected by the problems in a relationship. When a woman attempts to forgive too quickly, she may feel a lingering guilt or feeling of unworthiness. If she first takes time to explore the four healing emotions, she is then able to forgive her partner without bearing the unhealthy burden of guilt.

> When a relationship fails, men get most
> stuck by blaming their partner, while
> women blame themselves.

After finding forgiveness without bearing too much responsibility for the problems, the foundation has been laid for a woman to become fully accountable for her contribution to the problems in the relationship. With an attitude of forgiveness and responsibility, she is then empowered to move on with the self-assurance required to begin a new relationship. She is able to recognize that what she suffered in this relationship will not necessarily occur in the next.

An attitude of accountability empowers a woman to recognize that what she suffered in this relationship will not necessarily occur in the next.

If a woman equates having a relationship with sacrifice, then she will resist getting involved again. If a man remembers a past relationship with blame, he may continue to get involved, but when he is required to make normal sacrifices or compromises he is often quick to back out.

When we feel relief at the end of a relationship, our challenge is to continue looking at our feelings. A significant part of why we feel relief is that we can finally stop having all these uncomfortable feelings. Our tendency is to try to forget what happened. Certainly there are times when this strategy works, but it is not appropriate at the end of an intimate relationship.

By taking some time to explore our emotions beneath the surface feelings of relief, we will gradually find a whole world of unresolved feelings. Although we are happy to forget and to move on, it is wise to give ourselves permission to resent the whole experience and to feel all four healing emotions. When we don't have to forget our past to feel better, then we are ready to move into another relationship.

3. LETTING GO OF INDIFFERENCE

When a breakup does not fully involve our feelings, we run the risk of becoming too detached or indifferent. In trying to be reasonable, we run the risk of suppressing our feelings of loss. Since the mind adjusts faster than the heart, a "reasonable" breakup presents a challenge. When two people decide reasonably to end an intimate relationship or a marriage, in their hearts they may still be attached.

Ultimately, whenever a relationship ends we hope it is also a reasonable decision, but our challenge is also to feel our regrets. After deciding to break up, we must then give ourselves permission to feel reoccurring waves of conflicting emotions. Otherwise, we may lose touch with our inner passion to love and be loved.

Even though we are better off being apart, we must still take time to grieve the loss. We must recognize that some part of us was hoping that this relationship would last. That part of us needs to be heard again and again until the heart is healed.

It can be difficult to feel the four
healing emotions when a breakup is
the best solution.

When we end a relationship reasonably, we must make sure we give our feelings permission to lag behind. It is okay to regret the loss and feel sad even though it was the best decision. Even if breaking up is smartest decision, we still need to give ourselves a chance to adjust emotionally. If we do not automatically experience feelings of loss, we should begin to look for them.

You can achieve this by remembering the hopes and dreams you felt in the beginning of the relationship. With this awareness, you can begin to feel your sadness about breaking up. From here you can reflect on what happened that you didn't want to happen and explore feelings of anger and then forgiveness.

You must feel your fear that you could be making a big mistake and your sorrow that you cannot make it work. It is okay if you continue to feel occasional longings to go back and make it work. This is all part of the process of letting go. Having these feelings does not mean that you should act on your feelings and go back. If you are feeling needy and desperate, then this is definitely not the time to consider returning.

By exploring our feelings of
attachment, we can then let go without
having to detach from our feelings.

Staying in touch with our feelings of loss, even though our mind clearly is not attached, allows us to keep our hearts open. Breaking up in a very reasonable or detached manner can easily be covering up a lifetime of hidden hurt, disappointment, and sadness. If you are unable to find a way into your feelings of loss, then it is advisable to look back to another loss in your life. Somewhere in your past, something happened that blocked your ability to feel fully your need for love.

Breaking up in a very reasonable
manner can easily be covering up a
lifetime of disappointment and sadness.

Go back and remember a time when you were young but you had to be strong. A time when there was no one you could turn to. A time when you didn't feel safe to share your pain and so you made the reasonable decision to hold it in until it was finally safe. Well, now is the time to explore those feelings. Now it is safe. By getting in touch with each of the four levels and then fully feeling your forgiveness and love you will be ready to move on.

4. LETTING GO OF GUILT

When a relationship ends, there are generally two kinds of guilt we may feel. We feel guilty for all the possible ways we have hurt and disappointed our partner, or we feel guilty because we are ending the relationship. We promised our love and now we are breaking our promise. Whether we feel one or both types of guilt, the solution is the same—to release guilt our challenge is to forgive ourselves.

Although feeling guilty is a normal response to making a mistake, it is not healthy when we continue to feel guilty after recognizing our mistake. Guilt becomes toxic when we hear its message but then cannot release it with self-forgiveness. Guilt is toxic when it prevents us from feeling good about ourselves and our lives.

Just as some people hold on to feeling hurt in response to an injustice, others may hold on to feeling guilty for what they have done or not done. Feeling hurt and guilty are inextricably connected because the antidote for both is forgiveness. To release our hurt, we must forgive another. To release our guilt, we must forgive ourselves.

To the extent that we have not yet
learned to forgive others, it is more
difficult to forgive ourselves.

When we feel guilty after ending a relationship, it is a clear sign that we have not yet healed our hearts. Quite often, we are unable to forgive ourselves until we feel that others can forgive us.

It is not necessary that our ex-partner forgives us. It would be too limiting to think that our ex must forgive us before we can feel good about ourselves. It is helpful to write an in-depth apology letter sharing your mistakes and hoping that one day your ex can forgive you. In the meantime, it is most useful to find a therapist or support group and begin to share all that you feel guilty about.

Their nonjudgmental and accepting response will help you forgive yourself.

Forgiving ourselves is not
dependent on being forgiven.

Usually, when clients feel guilty about leaving a partner, they too have been left in their past. They personally know the pain of rejection and abandonment, and so they feel particularly guilty for inflicting that pain on another. When this guilt emerges, it is because their own pain of being left is still unresolved.

When we cannot forgive ourselves for hurting another, it is a clear indicator that we have been hurt in our past, but we haven't yet released the four healing emotions and resolved the hurt with forgiveness. If we feel guilt in leaving a partner, it is a very useful exercise to remember times in our past when we have been left or hurt.

By forgiving those who have hurt us,
we are then able to forgive ourselves
for having hurt another.

Some people hold on to guilt because they believe that they are bad and should feel guilty for leaving a partner who feels hurt, betrayed, or abandoned. This is incorrect thinking. If we realize that a relationship is not right for us, then it cannot be right for our partner. The greatest gift we can give someone is the opportunity to find love. If we are unable to get what we need in a relationship, then we can never give another what he needs. We will feel too resentful. Only by leaving him will he be free to find the love he needs.

Sometimes even when we are the ones who are the victims, we feel guilty for leaving. We may mistakenly feel sorry for our partners, when really they should be feeling sorry for the ways they have hurt us. This tendency to feel guilty is the result of suppressing the four healing emotions.

There are basically four ways our minds will suppress our emotional reactions to cause us to feel guilty about leaving. They are denial, justification, rationalization, and self-blame. Let's look at each in greater detail.

- **Denial**
  We say to ourselves that our partner really didn't mistreat us. We ignore what happened. To overcome being stuck in denial, we need to feel our anger. Anger reveals what happened that we didn't want, which we might otherwise overlook.

- **Justification**
  We defend what happened by making excuses for our partner. We might say, "Well, he didn't mean to do it." To overcome being stuck in justification, we need to feel our sadness. Sadness reveals what didn't happen that we wanted to happen. Sadness reminds us of what we are not getting instead of focusing on the reasons he didn't support us.

- **Rationalization**

  We tell ourselves that what happened really doesn't matter so much for a variety of reasons. We might say, "It could be much worse." To overcome being stuck in rationalizations, we need to feel our fear of never getting what we want and need. Fear reveals to us what could happen that we do not want to happen. It helps us to recognize what is important to us and not just what is important to our partner.

- **Self-Blame**

  We blame ourselves for provoking unwanted behavior. We might say, "If I had approached him differently, then he would not have . . ." Or "She did that, but I did this." To overcome being stuck in self-blame, we need to feel our sorrow. Sorrow assists us in recognizing what we cannot change. By feeling powerless to change our partner, we stop imagining that we are responsible for his or her mistreatment.

When these four tendencies prevent us from feeling our negative emotions, they are a problem. By taking the time to explore our negative feelings, we can clearly recognize the truth of a situation. Then we can make a decision to leave without feeling bad or guilty.

It is never a loving act to allow a person the opportunity to hurt us. If we are not getting what we need, then the most loving behavior is to end a relationship. If we discover that we do not feel our partner is right for us, then it is time to move on. Rather than end the relationship because our partner is inadequate or abusive in some way, end the relationship with forgiveness, but also with a recognition that he is not the right person for you.

5. LETTING GO OF INSECURITY

When a relationship ends, we cling to the hope of reconciliation sometimes to cope with our fears and insecurity. This holding onto hope protects us from having to confront our fears and from feeling the depth of our loss. As long as we believe we may get back together, we do not have to consider starting over. Although we may experience some relief, living in the hope of getting back together actually prevents us from completing the healing process. Living in hope prevents us from facing our fears and then letting go of our insecurity.

Even if there really is some hope of reconciliation, the best way to open that door is first to acknowledge emotionally that right now it is not only closed, but locked. We need to let go of hope in order to feel fully and release our pain. Although this is the best thing we can do for ourselves, it is also the best way to unlock the door of reconciliation.

If we are holding on to our hurt,
it can easily prevent our partner
from deciding to return.

When a relationship ends, it can only be rebuilt on a new foundation of understanding and forgiveness. As long as we are holding on to our hurt, then we have not fully forgiven our partner. When we continue to hurt, it can cause our partner to continue feeling guilt. Anything we say or do to make him feel guilty will only make it more difficult for him to find a desire to return.

If reconciliation is to happen, both partners must change or correct themselves in some way. By fully grieving the end of a relationship, we are eventually able to release our hurt with forgiveness, understanding, and gratitude. By releasing our pain, we are able to find an inner strength and trust that we can get the love we need.

With this new unattached awareness, we are no longer needy, desperate, clingy, anxious, or insecure. In this healthy state of mind and heart, we are then capable of making the necessary adjustments in ourselves either to attract our partner back or to recognize that she is not right for us. By successfully grieving the end of a relationship, we are able either to reconcile or to find a new and better relationship for ourselves.

6. LETTING GO OF HOPELESSNESS

Sometimes if we have been victims of abuse, neglect, deception, deprivation, abandonment, or betrayal, we can continue to feel like victims when a relationship ends. Though it is certainly true that we have been victimized, by ending the relationship, we are now free to get what we need. We are no longer victims, but fully responsible once again for what we get.

Although in our minds we recognize that we are no longer victims, we may still *feel* as if we are victims. As a result, we feel hopeless to ever get what we need and deserve. Unless we learn to let go of this hopelessness, we will not be motivated to make the right choices to find love.

Although we have taken action to
protect ourselves, we may continue
to feel like victims.

This tendency to feel like a victim is understandable, but unless we get help to heal our hurt, it is not healthy. Feeling hopeless is a clear indication that we have layers and layers of unresolved pain. Our challenge is to heal our hurt and find our ability to trust again. Without an understanding of how to release our pain, this attitude can be so strong that for the rest of our lives we feel we are still being victimized by our past. These are some examples of unhealthy victim thinking:

Because of what happened I will never be
    happy.
Because of what happened my life is ruined.
Because of what happened I wasted my life.
Because of what happened I will never be
    able to love again.

Because of what happened I will never be
   able to trust again.

Because of what happened I am too tired to
   start over.

Because of what happened I am not willing to
   be loving.

Because of what happened I am too bitter
   ever to love again.

Because of what happened I have nothing
   left to give.

I am unhappy today because of what
   happened.

I cannot trust again because of what
   happened.

I am alone today and will never find love
   because of what happened.

I will always resent what happened.

My best years are gone. I have no chance of
   finding love.

Rather than being limited by these beliefs, we
can use them as a springboard for diving into the
pool of our unresolved feelings. For example, if I
am believing that "I will never love again," then I
can take time to explore my feelings of fear. From
there I can look at other times in my life when I
could have had similar fears.

We can use our negative beliefs
as a flashlight to discover the
unresolved feelings hidden in the
closet of our unconscious.

Certainly, during the healing process it is understandable to have many of the above beliefs, but our goal is to identify incorrect thinking. By recognizing that we are caught in victim beliefs, we can begin to process the negative emotions associated with these beliefs. By triggering our inner healing response, our intuitive wisdom, receptivity, and creativity are automatically accessed. By turning on the light of our inner wisdom, the darkness of these victim beliefs is dispelled.

When we continue to blame our past for our pain, then the pain we feel today has everything to do with our past and nothing to do with our present reality. The unresolved pain from our past prevents us from fully experiencing the possibilities of the present. Until we heal our hearts, we will be unable to reach our inner power to create a new life. Instead, to various degrees, we will continue to suffer the pain of our past. Continuing to feel like victims, we are unable to fully embrace our lives.

7. LETTING GO OF JEALOUSY AND ENVY

When a marriage or relationship ends, sometimes our reaction is jealousy. Besides being a thorn in our side, jealousy prevents us from sharing in the good fortune of others. Although jealousy does block our ability to love, it is still important to identify so that we can work to heal it.

Jealousy and envy come up in a variety of ways. A few examples are listed below:

- We discover that our ex-partner is happy or having a good time. We may suddenly feel irritated or annoyed. Our annoyance comes from jealousy.

- When our children or others say good things about our ex-partner, we may begin to feel uncomfortable. Our discomfort comes from envy.

- When we imagine our ex-partner enjoying and loving someone else, we feel excluded and hurt. Our hurt comes from jealousy.

- Their happiness makes us miserable, while their misery brings us delight. Our glee and our misery both come from jealousy.

- If we see a couple in love we begin to think, It won't last. Our cynical attitude comes from envy.

Jealousy has many expressions and ways that it makes our life miserable. Rather than suffer the symptoms of jealousy, we can use it to heal ourselves. Jealousy is a clear indicator that we are denying a host of unfulfilled desires and ignoring our unresolved feelings.

**When we are envious, another's
happiness makes us miserable, while
their misery brings us delight.**

Jealousy arises when someone else has what we are wanting. Instead of feeling, "Yes, that's for me!" we resent their having it and not us. Envy arises when we tell ourselves that we are happy with what we have when really we are not and we want more. It is like a pointer that helps us to discover what we are hiding from ourselves. If I am envious of another's success, then I am wanting more success. If I am jealous that another is being loved or acknowledged, then I too am wanting to be loved. Jealousy and envy reveal what we are secretly wanting.

When we want something but believe we cannot have it, one of the ways to avoid feeling the pain of disappointment is to minimize the want or even deny it. We reason, "If I can't have it then it really isn't that important. I didn't want it anyway." If some hidden part of us is still wanting it, when someone else gets it, we are jealous.

Unless we are able to share in the happiness and success of others, our chances of being happy and fulfilled are diminished. As long as we feel jealous or envious, we are actually pushing away the very thing we want in life. Envy is clearly a sign that we are denying our potential to manifest what we want in life.

**As long as we feel envious
we are actually pushing away
the very thing we want in life.**

Jealousy is one of the most agonizing emotional states. Like each of the other six negative attitudes, the more we feel jealousy, the more painful and agonizing it becomes. Unlike the healing emotions of anger, sadness, fear, and sorrow, simply feeling the negative attitudes does not make them go away.

A touch of envy says, "You have what I want," but painful jealousy says, "You have what I want and I am in pain because I do not have it." Envy is actually a great guide that reveals where within ourselves we need to process our feelings and release our pain. If we do not confront and heal these deeper feelings, we will unknowingly obstruct or push away the very love, happiness, and success that we want.

Rather than being caught in the grip of jealousy, we can use this negative attitude to feel our deeper healing emotions. Let's say you are feeling jealous that your ex-partner is getting remarried. Rather than being jealous, uncomfortable, resentful, or critical, you could explore or write out the following kinds of feelings.

AN EXPLORATION OF FEELINGS UNDERLYING JEALOUSY

1. *Fear*

   I am afraid that I will not find the right person for me.

   I am afraid that I am not doing the right things.

   I am afraid that I am not good enough.

   I am afraid that others will think I was the problem in our marriage.

I am afraid that I don't know what to do to find love.

I am afraid that I am making a big mistake.

I am afraid no one will want me.

2. *Sadness*

I am sad that I am not getting married again.

I am sad that I am not so happy in my life.

I am sad that our marriage broke up.

I am sad that no one wants me.

I am sad that I am not happy right now.

I am sad that I am still unmarried.

I am sad that I have not found someone for me.

3. *Anger*

I am angry that I am still single.

I am angry that our marriage ended.

I am angry that they are happy and I am not.

I am angry that I am still looking for love.

I am angry that I have to start over.

I am angry that they are getting the attention and not me.

I am angry that when we were married he (she) wasn't so open.

4. *Sorrow*

I am sorry that I can't be happy for them.

I am sorry that I can't trust love.

I am sorry that our marriage failed.

I am sorry that I am not the one getting
   married.

I am sorry that I can't find the right person
   for me.

I am sorry that I can't find someone who
   loves me that way.

5. *Intention*

I want to get married again.

I want to find love.

I want to forgive my ex-partner.

I don't want to be so critical and jealous.

I want to love again.

I want to trust love.

I want to get married.

I want to feel good and happy again.

6. *Positive feelings of forgiveness, understanding,*
   gratitude, and trust

I forgive my ex for hurting me.

I forgive my ex for betraying me.

I forgive my ex for changing and not loving
   me anymore.

I forgive all my friends for liking him, too.

I understand that he deserves to be happy.

I understand that we were just not right for
   each other.

I am grateful for the opportunity to find
   love again.

I am grateful for the love I do have in my
   life.

I am grateful for my friends and family.
I trust that I will find love again.
I trust that I am in the process of getting
    everything that I need.
I trust that I will get the love that I want.

In this example, rather than be caught up in feelings of jealousy, a person can go a little deeper to feel the deeper emotions bottled up inside. After exploring the negative feelings, then the bottled-up positive feelings have a chance to come up as well.

HEALING OUR PAST

Rather than be limited by the seven negative attitudes, we can use them to discover and heal the unresolved feelings in our heart. As long as we are stuck in any of these seven attitudes we are not yet ready to get involved again. To experience the limitless possibilities for love and happiness that are available, we must be able to heal the wounds of our past. When we can eventually release our pain regarding what already has happened, we can be open to experiencing the positive possibilities of what truly can happen for us.

When we eventually are able to celebrate the ending of a relationship and be grateful for the lessons we learned, we have fully released and healed our hearts. If we were mistreated in a relationship, then certainly we are not grateful for the mistreatment, but we are grateful for the strength and wisdom we have gained as a result of letting go and then healing our hearts. In the next chapter, we will explore in greater detail the dynamics of letting go of our hurt and pain.

10

LETTING GO OF HURT

Of all possible losses, a divorce can be the most difficult to grieve. It is more complicated than the death of a spouse. When a partner dies, we are forced to accept that we cannot bring him back. The end is final. We clearly recognize that we can no longer depend on his love and support. Surrendering to this reality, we are fully able to grieve our loss.

After a divorce, our partner still lives. It is more difficult to grieve our loss, because we may continue to feel hurt. We may resent the way our ex is treating us, or feel jealous of the love and support she may be getting from someone else. We may blame her for not giving us enough support, or we may resent having to continue dealing with her.

**To whatever degree we feel
we were mistreated, we may
continue to feel hurt.**

Feeling hurt is a sign that we have not yet fully let go of needing the emotional support of our former spouse. For example, if a stranger is rude to us, we care much less than if our ex-partner has been rude. Naturally, we have different expectations of a stranger. After a divorce, it takes time to adjust our expectations from marriage partner to ex-partner.

For years we have been giving of ourselves, expecting to receive back love and support. To the degree that we have not gotten back what we deserved, a part of us is still expecting something in return. We may feel he still owes us. Somewhere deep inside, we are still expecting a payback. Until we give up depending on him, we will continue to feel hurt by him.

Feeling hurt after a breakup is a sign that we have not let go of needing the emotional support of our ex.

Besides being a cause of discontent, feeling hurt is a clear indication that we are looking for love and support in the wrong direction. Each day we hold on to hurt, we are missing the opportunities that exist to receive the love and support we need.

Letting go of hurt frees us to start over and find the love we need and deserve. As long as we continue to depend on our partner for emotional support, instead of healing our hurt, we will be adding to it. Emotional dependence is fine when the support is available. When our partner's love and support is not available, we must let go of our dependence.

As long as we continue to depend on
our partner for emotional support, we
will only add to our hurt.

We cannot heal a broken bone if we don't first acknowledge that it is broken. By continuing to be emotionally dependent on our partner, we are not acknowledging the break. We are merely putting our feelings of loss on hold and denying our sorrow that we can no longer get what we need from them. Although we may find temporary relief, we will eventually begin to resent our partner's unwillingness to cooperate with what we want.

When our expectations are not satisfied and we feel hurt, we will begin to feel like victims. As long as we feel our partner is standing in the way of our happiness, we will continue to feel hurt by them. By becoming aware of how we set ourselves up to feel hurt we become free to change our attitude. These are some common examples of hurt feelings and the hidden victim thinking that perpetuates our hurt.

HURT FEELINGS AND VICTIM BELIEFS

The Hurt Feeling

The Victim Belief

I feel hurt that you didn't try harder to make things better.

If you had tried, I could be happy today.

I feel hurt that you did not consider getting help.

If you had gotten help, I could be happy today.

I feel hurt that you did not change for me.

If you would have changed, I could be happy today.

I feel hurt that you did not care about me.

If you had cared about my needs, I could be happy today.

I feel hurt that you changed so much.

If only you would change back, I could be happy today.

I feel hurt that you rejected me.

If only you would love me again, I could be happy today.

I feel hurt that you loved someone else and not me.

If only you would love me, I could be happy today.

I feel hurt that you ignored me.

If only you cared more, I could be happy today.

I feel hurt that you betrayed me; you didn't keep your promise.

If you had kept your promise, I could be happy today.

I feel hurt that you criticized me.

If only you had supported me, I could be happy today.

I feel hurt that you made a fool of me.

If you had respected me, I could be happy today.

I feel hurt that you abandoned me.

If you had stayed, I could be happy today.

By exploring our hurt feelings we are able to discern the victim attitudes associated with them. These hidden attitudes can actually prevent us from ever letting go of our hurt feelings. Instead of releasing our pain, a victim attitude reinforces the need to continue feeling pain.

LIVING IN PRESENT TIME

If we are to release our hurt, we must recognize that we cannot continue to depend on our partner. When a relationship ends, we must recognize that it is over. Our ex-partner is no longer responsible for our pain. The injury has occurred, but now it is up to us and not him to make things better. Yes, he may have caused our hurt, but now we are responsible for healing our feelings. It is we who are responsible for healing our broken heart, not him.

When we recognize that we are not dependent on our partner to be happy or fulfilled, she cannot continue to hurt us. When we are no longer being hurt by her, in the present, then we are free to release the hurt we are still carrying around. This is a very simple but profound concept. If there is nothing to worry about, I can let go of my worries or stop worrying. If there is nothing hurting me, I can let go of my hurt or stop feeling hurt. If in present time I am not being hurt, then I am most capable of letting go of any lingering past hurt that I feel.

By recognizing that we are not
dependent on our ex-partner, he or she
cannot continue to hurt us.

If our ex-partner continues to do things that annoy us, we must recognize that he is not breaking our heart. That has already happened. This is an important distinction. Let's imagine that you can measure a hurt in degrees as you can measure the temperature. On this imaginary scale, a little annoyance is 5 degrees while a broken heart is 100 degrees.

If your heart is healed and your ex-partner annoys you, then you might feel 5 degrees of hurt. But if your heart is still broken, then when your partner annoys you, it doesn't just hurt 5 degrees. Instead it forces you to feel the 100 degrees of pain from your broken heart and the extra 5 degrees.

Unless we are correctly able to interpret this distinction, we will believe that every time our partner annoys us she is breaking our hearts once more. Even though it feels as if our hurt is 105 degrees, we are really just connecting to our unresolved past hurt. Incorrectly believing that our partner is continuing to break our heart makes our pain much greater. If we do not take the time to heal our broken heart, the things she does that annoy or irritate us many seem unbearable.

As long as we believe we are being victimized in present time, we will continue to feel hurt. It is much more difficult to let go of hurt when we are being hurt. To release our hurt, we must live in present time, recognizing that the hurt we are seeking to release occurred in the past.

We can let go of our hurt by holding
an attitude that we *were* victims,
but that *now* we are not.

To heal a broken bone, after first acknowledging that it has been broken, we must then protect it from being hurt again. We cannot reset the bone straight if we keep breaking it. Likewise, we cannot reset our hearts with forgiveness, understanding, gratitude, and trust when we believe that we are still being victimized as before.

If we give our partner the power to
break our hearts over and over
then we will never heal.

These are some examples of releasing our victim attitude by living in present time:

- Yes, I have been disappointed and betrayed, but now I am free to change my desires and expectations.

- Yes, I was deprived of love, rejected, and abandoned, but now I am free to find it elsewhere.

- Yes, I am in pain, but the pain is no longer being inflicted on me.

- Yes, my heart has been broken, but now I am responsible to heal what has been done.

- Yes, I am feeling devastated, but in time I will find love again.

- Yes, I may have wasted time, but I have learned many valuable lessons. Now I can heal my broken heart and prepare myself to find true and lasting love.

THE TWO HANDS OF HEALING

There are basically two hands of healing, and both are required to heal our hearts. With one hand, we must give ourselves permission to feel what we feel. With the other hand, we must have a nonvictim attitude. To heal our hearts we must maintain a nonvictim attitude in present time while simultaneously experiencing the victim feelings of our past.

To heal our hurt we must feel it,
but also recognize that it belongs
to our past.

This healing attitude can best be understood using the image of a loving parent holding a child in his or her arms. The child is crying, saying, "I am so sad, no one will ever really love me." The parent doesn't interrupt and say, "That's ridiculous. You are loved and will always be loved." The compassionate parent just holds the child, understanding his pain and sadness. Then the parent reassures the child that he is loved.

In a similar way, when we are feeling like victims, one part of us needs to be the positive, responsible parent, but the other needs to be the child who is just a bundle of feelings that need to be expressed before clarity is found. Being the parent, we remain rooted in a nonvictim attitude. This perspective then frees us to keep letting go of the victim feelings that come up.

To let go of pain, we must learn
to maintain a nonvictim attitude,
while at the same time experiencing
our victim feelings.

To get a concrete sense of what this process is like, try this little experiment. Take a few minutes to practice doing two different things at the same time. Use your left hand to circle around your stomach clockwise and your right hand to pat your head at the same time.

Go ahead, try it right now. It's fun. It will only take a few minutes to practice. Don't read on until you have mastered it. If it is very easy, then try switching the hands or try circling your stomach counterclockwise.

With a little practice, it's not really that difficult, but it is definitely not automatic. It takes a deliberate intention. Similarly, dealing with our emotional pain is not really difficult. It too just takes a clear and deliberate intention. When we can simultaneously know we are no longer being victimized (patting the head) but also feel victim emotions (circling the stomach), then we have created the required healing attitude.

CREATING A HEALING ATTITUDE

Most people do not understand how to create a healing attitude. They either deny their victimlike feelings or they get lost in them and cannot let go. As a result they experience a host of undesirable emotional states. They are plagued by recurring feelings of hurt, jealousy, resentment, blame, indifference, hopelessness, insecurity, and guilt. As long as they do not heal their hearts they are unable to tap into their inner love, wisdom, receptivity, and creativity.

Unless we are able to maintain a healing attitude, simply talking about our feelings may make matters worse. If the listener simply agrees with our hurt, we may we end up feeling more bitter, depressed, or drained. Talking is not enough to heal our hearts. Sometimes just getting it out will bring some temporary relief, but there is no real or lasting healing.

Getting angry or complaining is not enough, unless we are also looking for forgiveness. Feeling hurt and sad will just give us a headache if we don't seek to find a deeper understanding and acceptance of what happened. Exploring our fears, worries, and doubts will only increase our insecurities if we are not also giving thanks for our blessings. Disclosing our feelings of shame, embarrassment, and sorrow will only increase our feelings of inadequacy, unworthiness, and guilt unless we are also learning to forgive ourselves.

We can create the right healing attitude to heal our hearts by taking time to explore our past feelings and to enrich them with the intent to find forgiveness, increase our understanding, give thanks, and trust again.

11

THE 90–10 PRINCIPLE

The pain we feel in present time is almost always linked to the unresolved pain of our past. When something hurts us in present time, then all the similar hurt from our past gets released as well. The unresolved and repressed feelings from our childhood or past relationships intensify the feelings of hurt we feel regarding our current loss. Much of the time, 90 percent of the hurt we feel in present time has to do with our past and only 10 percent has to do with what we think we are upset about. When we can't release our painful feelings, it is often because we are not upset for the reasons we think.

Only 10 percent of the hurt we feel
has to do with what we think
we are upset about.

We experience this 90–10 principle all the time. If we have had a terrible day and people have been rude to us, we were stuck in traffic and we have a headache, when we get home we also bring these unresolved feelings of the day. If our partner is rude to us she may get the brunt of our entire day. Her rudeness may be the straw that breaks the camel's back.

We become upset with our partner when really most of our upset has to do with the other events during the day. If we had a wonderful day and our partner was rude to us, it would be much easier to deal with. We would automatically be more understanding because we have had a good day and we are not carrying around a load of unresolved feelings about our day.

This same principle applies to suppressed feelings that extend all the way back to our childhood. When we are devastated by a loss, it triggers feelings from our past. When we get stuck in negative feelings like resentment, blame, indifference, guilt, insecurity, hopelessness, and jealousy, it is a clear indication that 90 percent of our hurt has to do with the past and only 10 percent has to do with the present.

When it is difficult to shake off our negative feelings, it is generally an indicator that we need to link our feelings in present time to feelings in our past. The healing process becomes much easier if we can relive the unresolved feelings of our past.

It is always easier to deal with past events than current events. When we look at our past we have the added advantage of knowing how things turned out. We have a greater objectivity to listen compassionately with a healing attitude. One part of us is in the pain, while another part of us is like a caring friend or a loving parent.

When we heal our past, we have the
added advantage of knowing how
things will turn out.

By feeling safe and supported to open up and share what surfaces regarding circumstances in present then automatically the past hurt can be identified. By linking the pain in the present to other times in which we have had similar feelings, a much more profound letting go can take place.

This approach has not only helped thousands of clients and participants in my healing workshops, but it has helped me personally in healing the ending of my first marriage.

HEALING THE PAST TO HEAL THE PRESENT

When I first met my wife Bonnie, we quickly fell in love. After about a year and a half of dating, I thought I wanted to marry her, but I just wasn't ready. Some part of me wasn't sure. I loved her, but I was ambivalent about getting married. I did not realize at the time that uncertainty is a normal part of the courting process. To keep a long story short, we decided to end our relationship.

Within three years, I went on to marry another woman who had been an old friend. We were both getting our doctorates in psychology together. We began teaching workshops on relationships. We were in love and eventually decided to get married. As we grew in love, we shared many of the lessons we were learning while trying to make our relationship work.

After being married for two years we started to break apart. The feelings of passion and attraction had gone away, and we began to wonder if we were right for each other. We decided to separate. By healing my heart, I was able to end my marriage with love and then recognize that Bonnie was the right woman for me.

THE DAY OF SEPARATION

I can still remember that day clearly. Although it was the right decision, I was very disappointed. I couldn't believe that it had come to this. I was so sad that our relationship was over. Although it was a mutual decision to end our marriage, a part of me still wanted her, loved her, and needed her. We were very attached. She was also devastated. We loved each other, but recognized that we were not right for each other.

I went out on my own, and just cried for hours. I would drive around and listen in my car to songs that we had enjoyed together. I grieved with buckets of tears. I didn't know where I was going to go or what I was going to do. I felt as if my life had crashed down around me. I felt like a failure in my marriage and also in my career. How could I counsel others or teach workshops on relationships when my own had failed?

I was so devastated that I called my mother. Normally, I would only call my mother to check in to see how she was doing or share with her good things that were going on in my life. It had been probably twenty years since I had cried in front of her or shared my grief.

When I talked to her on the phone, I asked her if she would come out to California. I was living in Los Angeles, and she was in Texas. She immediately said yes. She said her bags were packed to visit one of her grandchildren, and she was just on the way to the airport. She would change her ticket and take the next plane out.

As I waited for her in the airport, I began writing down all my feelings of loss. I knew that it was very important for me to get my feelings out. Not only would it help me in the long run, it also brought incredible relief. While in the process of writing out my sadness, I heard these very tender feelings deep inside saying, "Please don't leave me, please don't go." Along with these feelings came a memory from my childhood that I had forgotten.

LINKING THE PRESENT WITH THE PAST

When I was about six years old, my family went on a vacation from Texas to Los Angeles. All seven of us got into the station wagon and drove across the country to California. I was the youngest on that trip. We had rented a beach house for a month and were expecting to visit relatives who lived nearby.

We were all incredibly excited about going to visit Disneyland. After we arrived, our relatives visited us and invited any of us to visit them. One of my older brothers whispered in my ear that they lived next door to Disneyland. Well, I immediately volunteered. I thought everyone would want to come along.

When I arrived at my relatives', I was surprised that no one else had come along in another car. In retrospect, I realize that I was simply in shock. I could not believe that my mother wasn't there. I was all alone with strangers. I was there for a week, and we never went to Disneyland.

Children don't always recognize the opportunities that exist to find love and end up feeling powerless.

During those seven days, I didn't realize that I could have asked Aunt Innie to call my mother and have her pick me up. I thought my family had forgotten me. I thought I would never get back. I remember one day being furious inside. Defiantly, at six years old, I walked to the end of the block determined to leave this prison and find my family. At the end of the block, I realized that I didn't know where to go. Feeling defeated, I lowered my head and walked back.

RETURNING HOME

On the seventh day, one of my older cousins was teasing me and I started to cry. My aunt Innie looked at me and said, "You need your mommy." At that moment, I burst into hysterical tears. Nobody had realized how upset I had been about being separated from my family.

Aunt Innie said years later that she had never seen a child get so upset. She immediately brought me back to my family. She decided not to tell my mother what had happened because she didn't want to worry her. My mother sensed my insecurities and dedicated the next day to spend with me.

The next day on the beach I remember looking around and feeling really little. The world was suddenly a vast place, and I was very small. I wondered who all these people were, where they were going, and what they did. I wondered how I would ever make my way in this world.

The feeling from that day stayed with me throughout my life. Some part of me had always felt small and insecure; wondering how I would fit into this world. I thought that as I got older it would just go away. Even though I was in my thirties, a part of me still felt like that small, abandoned boy, powerless to get home.

Writing out my hurt feelings while waiting for my mother to arrive had released into my conscious mind this past memory. Up to that point in my life, I could always remember walking on the beach with my mother, but I had completely blocked the memory of being left with my relatives for seven days. I had no idea that I had felt so abandoned.

TRIGGERING REPRESSED MEMORIES AND EMOTIONS

The devastating loss of my failed marriage had awakened these past repressed feelings. As I waited for my mother, I vigorously began writing out the feelings that I had forgotten. I linked the feelings I was having in the present to my past. I then relived the experience by writing out my feelings. I enriched the experience by giving the six-year-old inside me the words and the ability to articulate his pain with each of the four healing emotions.

I gave voice to the feelings that had never been expressed or fully heard. Right there in the airport, tears rolled down my cheeks as this sad little boy who had lost his mother cried. He felt so alone, so abandoned, so hurt, so betrayed, so uncertain of what to do, so afraid that he would never see his family again.

In retrospect, it is easy to discount these feelings by acknowledging that the little boy was not really abandoned. But the little boy didn't know that. He felt as if he was on his own and there was no one to take care of him. He was angry that he had been left, he was sad that he was alone, he was afraid of being forgotten and unloved, and he was sorry that he couldn't get home. He felt inadequate, helpless, and lost.

After writing about my painful memories in this manner, I felt much better. About that time, my mother's plane arrived. I greeted her with a big hug and thanked her for coming. After I briefly explained that I had left my wife that day, I said, "I don't even know where we can stay."

Without any knowledge of the feelings I had just written, she said, "That's not a problem. We can stay with Aunt Innie." I couldn't believe it. Not only had I brought up this past memory to be healed and updated, I had the opportunity to go back to Aunt Innie's and relive being there, but this time with my mother.

RELIVING THE PAST

My mother stayed the whole week with me at Aunt Innie's. We went to Disneyland twice. I was still devastated, but I was able to share my feelings of loss directly with my mother. That was a long week. I feel so lucky that I could share it with someone who loved me. I still couldn't sleep at night and at times would have chills and shake. I was so sad, but I appreciated being so close with my mother. At times, I was really feeling the vulnerability of a six-year-old.

At the end of the seven days, the last night before my mother left, a celebrity client of mine invited me to his going-away party. He was dying of cancer and he had invited all his friends. He wanted to say good-bye to them and celebrate the special love they had shared. (He died a month later.)

At the party, I was being introduced to various celebrities who were there. I generally felt a little insecure when I was around famous people. On this particular evening it was different. I had just been through a week of torture, and so this seemed easy. I remember standing beside my mother while I was being introduced to a celebrity. As I introduced my mother, I looked over to her and realized for the first time in my life that I was taller than she.

After a week of healing, I looked over and realized for the first time in my life that I was taller than my mother.

I had always felt as if she was taller than I. For the first time in my life, I felt grown up. The six-year-old boy inside me had finally had a chance to grow up. Although I was thirty-four years old, a part of me had always felt like that little six-year-old walking on the beach with his mother, holding her hand, wondering how he would ever manage to fit into this huge world.

BECOMING WHOLE AGAIN

Ironically, allowing myself to feel the emotions and thoughts of the wounded six-year-old inside me enabled me to grow up. If children are not able to express their feelings and be heard with love and compassion when they experience trauma, their feelings become repressed. It is as if some part of who they are freezes. That forgotten part doesn't get the chance to grow up until some event in the future warrants feeling that level of pain. Then the past pain becomes triggered, and we have a chance to heal it and become whole.

After this healing, I realized that I had been attracted to my first wife not by mistake or by poor judgment, but because some part of me was still repressed and needed to heal. After healing my past, I was then free to find lasting love in my life. After about a year of healing, I was finally able to recognize that Bonnie was the right woman for me, and we have been happily married ever since. In the next chapter, we will explore in greater detail the process of healing our past.

12

PROCESSING OUR HOT SPOTS

Besides learning to process the four healing emotions, one of the easiest and most powerful ways to heal the heart and release our pain is to link the hurt we feel in present time with the hurt we felt in our past. By linking our current painful feelings with unresolved feelings in our past, we can process these hot spots in our past and be free of the pain we feel in the present.

This one concept is at the basis of all forms of therapy and healing throughout the world. By talking about our past, we are able to remember our pain rather than feeling as if we are still being hurt. The more we can recall our pain, the less it is able to grip us in present time. There is a big difference between feeling "I was hurt" and feeling "I am being hurt."

This does not mean that we should not feel our hurt. It just means that dwelling on our hurt is not very helpful. Instead, we should use our hurt feelings as a springboard to dive into the pool of our past unresolved emotions. We should feel our hurt, but also recognize that it is merely an indicator that our emotions about a particular incident in our past are still unresolved. Ideally we should use our hurt feelings to lead us to the pain we still need to heal.

THREE STEPS OF HEALING

To accomplish our healing three steps are required.

In step one, we need to link our feelings in present time with those in our past. If I am feeling hurt that I was rejected today, then I recall when I felt rejected in my past.

Step two is reliving the incident. After first recalling an incident, I then imagine that I am back at that time experiencing what happened.

Step three is enriching the incident. While reliving the incident, I give myself the benefit of resources that I now have that I didn't have then. I imagine that I can share my feelings with a loving parent, friend, or angel, and process my hurt by practicing the three parts of the Feeling Better Exercise.

Instead of feeling hurt that I was rejected, I link this hurt to the hurt I felt in my past by recalling what happened to make me feel rejected. Then I relive the incident by imagining that I am in the past experiencing the rejection. This time I can take the time to enrich the experience. As I relive the event I can stop it any moment to enrich the experience by exploring all of the deeper facets of my experience I might have missed. At any moment, I can choose to process a particular feeling more deeply and to attempt to find forgiveness, greater understanding, gratitude, and trust.

Reliving an event is just like watching a video. At any moment we can put the video on pause. Recalling a particular circumstance, I can "freeze-frame" my experience at any painful moment and then heal the pain by exploring the four healing emotions. We can exercise our ability to enrich the experience by exploring more deeply each of the four healing emotions as well as giving ourselves the support we didn't get at that time.

SHARING OUR HURT

Sharing our feelings with a friend, counselor, or support group helps us to move through these three steps of healing. While talking about our past, our current feelings are linked to our past. To the degree that others can relate to our pain, we will automatically begin to relive the experience. To the extent that others have experienced and healed similar pain our ability to heal our pain is greatly enriched. In this case, the automatic healing process is greatly nurtured through sharing our pain with others.

Just as the support of others may facilitate our healing, it may also block it. If others are giving us too much advice rather than simply listening, we may remain disconnected to our true feelings and become stuck. To feel our pain, we must feel safe. We cannot be concerned that someone will minimize or judge our feelings or use them against us in any way. We must be assured that everything we share will remain confidential. When these conditions are met, the process of healing is enormously facilitated.

The safety to share our feelings is one of the biggest elements in healing. As adults, we suppress certain feelings because as children it was not completely safe to express our emotions. The automatic ways we cope with emotions as adults were actually learned at a very early age. When it was not safe to express particular emotions as children, we learned to cope with stressful situations by suppressing what we felt.

As children, our feelings often came up at the most inconvenient times. Our parents, caretakers, and siblings generally did not have the time or the skill to hear us with a healing attitude. Without the safety to express and explore our feelings as children, we did not fully learn how to move through negative emotions to find the positive feelings of forgiveness, understanding, acceptance, gratitude, and trust.

As adults, we can choose to create a supportive environment to heal our pain. We can choose friends who are not judgmental and support groups and counselors who can assist us in discovering and exploring what we feel. It is never too late to learn how to transform negative emotion into positive emotion. With the insight into what is required to heal a broken heart, you can not only survive a loss, but grow tremendously.

THE MANY LAYERS OF HEALING

As soon as we feel we are over our loss, it is not uncommon to experience setbacks. After feeling better we may again experience any of the basic symptoms of suppression: hurt, resentment, blame, indifference, guilt, insecurity, hopelessness, and jealousy. Even though we are making progress, until we have fully healed our hearts, these and other symptoms of unresolved feelings may come up repeatedly.

Healing the heart occurs in many layers. It is similar to the process of peeling an onion. After peeling one layer of our hurt, we are then faced with the next layer to peel. In practical terms this means that after feeling loving and forgiving for a while, we may then begin to feel jealous or resentful once again.

Healing the heart is a gradual process
of unfoldment, one layer at a time.

After feeling confident and assured that we will find love, we may become anxious or doubtful, or even begin to miss our partner. After feeling really good about ourselves we may feel guilty, inadequate, or unworthy of love. Suddenly, as if for no reason at all, we may begin to feel disconnected from our warm loving feelings and instead experience an empty numbness. These are not really setbacks, but examples of progressing to the next layer of healing.

It takes time to heal a loss fully. For each two steps of progress, we may experience one step back. Although it might seem like a setback, it really isn't. We are just getting to a deeper level of healing.

Each time we think we are through
our healing, we really have
just healed one layer.

It is important to recognize this pattern of healing one layer at a time, otherwise we may misinterpret our progress. We may become discouraged and give up the process of deliberately exploring our feelings. Instead of coping with our loss through healing our feelings, we may seek the temporary relief of suppressing our feelings, but as a consequence suffer the symptoms of suppression for a lifetime.

FINDING OUR MISSING FEELINGS

When we experience any of the symptoms of suppression, it is because we are suppressing one or more of the four healing emotions: anger, sadness, fear, or sorrow. To heal our hurt, we must counteract a lifetime habit of suppressing certain emotions and find the missing feelings. When we have been suppressing certain feelings since childhood, it can be very difficult to recover them on our own.

Earlier today, I mistakenly closed this file without saving my work. As a result, two pages of writing that were not yet saved were lost. Fortunately, I have a backup system that recovers any lost or deleted files. Without that backup system, I would have completely lost the unsaved material. In a similar manner, while growing up, we delete certain emotional reactions or files. Until we are able to recover these lost files, our ability to heal our hurt will be limited.

**We all have a backup system
to recover lost memories that
need to be healed.**

For example, if I have a tendency since childhood to suppress angry feelings, then my ability to feel and release my anger as an adult will be limited. That could cause me to remain stuck in fear, sorrow, or sadness for a lifetime. As a result, I may occasionally experience jealousy, guilt, or any of the other symptoms of suppression. To the extent that I have suppressed feelings of anger in my past, it will be difficult to feel appropriate anger regarding my current loss. This same analysis applies equally to the suppression of any of our emotions.

Seeking out help is like using a backup system

for finding any lost or deleted experiences. All we
need is someone to trigger our memory. Brain sur-
geons have discovered that by stimulating parts of
the brain, they can randomly trigger vivid memories of the past that were completely forgotten by
the patient. Fortunately our unresolved and hidden feelings can be triggered without brain
surgery.

By sharing our pain
with others our hidden memories
can be recovered.

Our feelings are suppressed because in the past
it was not safe or useful to express them. As long
as we hold the belief that we cannot share our
thoughts, feelings or desires, we can be assured
that within ourselves certain feelings are also
being suppressed. Certainly it is not safe to share
ourselves fully with just anybody. It is a wise decision to hold back our inner world of thoughts,
feelings, hopes, and dreams when someone will
not be supportive of us.

By establishing a healing
relationship with a counselor or
support group, you will eventually feel
safe enough to share all of you.

If we want to gain the ability to open our heart
fully to experience love, wisdom, receptivity, and

creativity, then it is our responsibility to create a
safe setting to explore and share both our present
feelings and our past feelings.

HOW TO PROCESS OUR PAST

By linking the pain you feel in the present with
past pain, you can most effectively release any
past repressed feelings that are limiting your ability to feel and release pain in the present. For
example, if you have unresolved fear from a past
experience, it will block you from releasing your
fear in present time. If in present time you are
unable to fully experience and release your fears,
then you may become stuck in your ability to
move through your negative feelings to experience
your positive feelings.

An unresolved fear from a past
experience will block you from
releasing your fear in present time.

To use the power of remembering, practice
these exercises to assist you in linking your present feeling back to your past. Put on some soothing background music and ask yourself these
questions. Listen for the answers that come up.
Take any memory and explore it even if it is not
the correct answer to the question. If the question
is "Remember when you were loved," you may
remember when you were not loved. This is nor-

mal and to be expected. When a painful memory comes up, pounce on it.

HOW TO REMEMBER

Take time to relive that memory and then enrich it using the Feeling Better Exercise. Don't get caught up in trying to remember clearly or to visualize. Even a faint or vague memory is fine. Once you have an idea of the situation, then imagine what you might have felt. Imagine that you felt then the same feelings you are having in present time. As you get good at this, instead of being unable or afraid to remember your past, it will become your supportive friend.

Even a faint or vague memory is
enough to process our past.

Never feel as if you can't reprocess an event. It is fine to use a particular memory again and again. Each time we process a particular event, we are not just opening an old wound, we are increasing our ability to release pain with forgiveness, understanding, gratitude, and trust.

By going back and remembering what was difficult to forgive, and then finding forgiveness, you strengthen your ability to forgive. The next time you go back, even though you have already found forgiveness, go back to before you had found forgiveness and go through the process again. Each time you repeat the process, you will increase your ability to forgive and resolve pain with positive feelings.

Healing past feelings strengthens
our ability to forgive, give thanks,
and trust in present time.

When it is difficult to forgive something in present time rather than struggle with it, go back to an event in your past that was hard to forgive and process it. By linking your present pain to that past event and then reliving it with forgiveness, you will release the pain of not forgiving in the present. When you return to present time, you will be able to easily find forgiveness.

It is also advisable to be open to new memories as well. By healing one past memory, other pain is drawn up that needs to be healed. If you can't remember your childhood, then start by remembering something from a few years ago or whenever. By processing whatever you can remember, you will begin to remember other things as well.

To assist you in this process, get out a photo album and look at pictures to help you trigger your memories. It doesn't matter how accurate your memories are. If you cannot directly remember, imagine what you would remember if you could. Although it may not be accurate, it will work just as well. What you imagine will link you to your past feelings.

LOOKING FOR POSITIVE MEMORIES

Most of the processing questions are looking for positive experiences. By asking questions to evoke positive experiences, you are supported by your past. Meanwhile, any painful experiences that need to healed will automatically be remembered.

When Lisa was asked to remember a time she felt loved by her father, she remembered a time when her father didn't keep a promise and hurt her feelings. When Kevin was asked to remember when he felt his mother's love, he first remembered driving in the car with her to have lunch. He felt special having time with her. After exploring the question again, he remembered waiting for hours to be picked up from elementary school. This time a flood of sad and hurt feelings began to come up. He was then able to link his current feelings of abandonment with the sadness he felt when his mother forgot to pick him up.

The result of dealing with unresolved feelings from the past is a greater memory and connection to our positive feelings that were repressed along with the negative feelings.

The more we are able to uncover
the negative memories, the positive
memories become stronger
and more clear.

After Kevin healed his sadness about being forgotten by also feeling fear, sorrow, and anger, he was then able to feel the special love he felt at that time for his mother. Remembering when he fully loved and needed his parents opened him to feeling more loved and supported in present time. Even though he felt rejected by his ex-partner, he was better able to feel the support of his friends and family.

After processing her hot spot and forgiving her father, Lisa was able to remember her innocent and trusting feelings. By forgiving her father, her ability to forgive herself increased. Although in present time she was feeling guilty for ending a relationship, she was now finding relief and healing by experiencing the innocence she felt as a child. By processing her past hot spot, she was able to release present feelings of shame, guilt, and inadequacy.

By remembering positive experiences and processing hot spots, we can connect with all the positive feelings that may have been repressed. We can remember being fully alive and present, full of love and joy. It is not that we want to be children again, but be as children—be responsible adults in touch with our ability to love, our joy, and our creativity.

When we can recover all the positive feelings of innocence and be an experienced and wise adult, we are whole. We do not need to develop positive aspects of our character, we just need to uncover and recover these positive attributes of who we were. By healing the pain of our past, then we have so much more love to heal the pain in the present.

TAKE WHATEVER COMES UP

After asking a question, work with whatever comes to mind. If something comes up that you don't want to deal with, then don't. Simply move on to another question. You don't have to deal with everything right away. Eventually, after healing your heart, you will easily be able to deal with and heal anything that comes up.

The point of these questions is not to dig up painful memories. If you are in a good mood or feeling happy, then don't bother looking into the past. These processes are designed to assist you in letting go of pain in the present by linking it to our past experiences. By remembering positive moments when we overcame challenges in our past, we are able to let go of pain and meet our challenges in the present.

The point of these questions is
not to dig up painful memories
but to draw support from
our past successes.

In a sense, we are getting two birds with one stone. We are healing any past issues that may be affecting or intensifying how we feel in present time. And by reconnecting with the positive feelings of our past, we are able to draw support to resolve our issues in the present.

This list of questions can also be used in a counseling session or in a workshop setting. In a workshop or support group, you could pair up with a partner and take turns asking each other a question from the list, talking about the memories that come up. When you discover a hot spot, a memory with emotional charge, then you can stop and process it by role-playing the feeling better exercise.

In counseling or in a workshop, as you relive a hot spot from your past, you can then enrich your experience by exploring and expressing the four healing feelings. Your partner or therapist can then ask questions according to the feeling better format, the response letter format, and the completion letter format. By sticking to the format, unnecessary tangents and discussions are avoided. Discussion is appropriate after the process.

In counseling or in a workshop,
you can relive and then heal a
hot spot from your past.

With your eyes closed, pretend you are in the past answering the suggested questions. Once you have finished, it can be helpful to role-play the response that you wanted to hear. After you come up with the response you needed to hear in your past, then your partner gives a version of that response while you keep your eyes closed.

As you hear the words you needed to hear, imagine how you would have felt. Pretend that it is really happening. Give yourself permission to feel your reaction to the love you deserved to receive. By letting in this love, you will automatically uncover your positive feelings that were repressed as well.

Although we cannot change the past, we can give ourselves the real experience of how we would have felt if someone had listened to us and been there for us. To heal our heart we don't need to change our past, we just need to give ourselves the love and support that was missing so that we can uncover the positive feelings of love, trust, joy, appreciation, confidence, excitement, enthusiasm, and so on that were repressed along with the negative feelings.

DEVELOPING IMPORTANT SKILLS

Besides assisting us in uncovering our positive feelings, processing our hot spots gives us the ability to exercise and develop important skills that were not fully developed. This is a list of some of the important skills that need to developed in childhood.

- Forgiveness
- Self-forgiveness
- Respecting others
- Respecting ourselves
- Offering help
- Asking for help

- Sharing our feelings appropriately
- Clearly articulating our thoughts, feelings, and wants
- Hearing others with empathy and compassion
- Patience
- Self-correction
- Delaying gratification
- Cooperating with others
- Sharing credit
- Sharing success with others
- Receiving acknowledgment and praise
- Giving acknowledgment and praise
- Taking calculated risks
- Conscience; recognizing what is good and bad
- Honesty
- Recognizing our worth and valuing others
- Creative problem-solving
- Accepting what can't be changed
- Thinking for ourselves and from our hearts
- Taking responsibility for our actions and our feelings
- Selfless giving and setting healthy boundaries

After reading this list, you will reflect that most adults have not learned all these skills. Yet it is never too late. By taking the time to heal your heart, you will get the additional benefit of developing these important skills for living. By taking the time to heal your past while healing your present loss, you will uncover your potential to develop each of these skills. By doing the exercises again and again, you will actually be developing each of the above skills.

EXERCISES FOR REMEMBERING

Ask yourself these questions and take the answers that come up. After recalling an event, remember the beginning, middle, and end of each experience. Then go back further in time and remember an earlier event. Repeat a question two or three times. When nothing else comes up, then move on to the next question. Remembering positive memories in this way is comforting when we are in pain.

If painful or negative memories begin to come up, welcome them as well. By linking the pain you feel in present time to a past memory, you can more effectively heal it. Once this hot spot or painful memory is identified, then it is time to process it using the feeling better exercise.

Each time you ask a question again, go back a little further in time. Eventually try to remember the earliest memory. If the question is "Recall going to school," then eventually try to remember

your first day of school. Please don't feel confined
to any part of the list. You can start at the beginning or you can skip around. You can answer
questions again and again.

PROCESS QUESTIONS FOR STARTING OVER

Recall when you eventually succeeded.

Recall when you were confident.

Recall when you were scared, but found
safety.

Recall when you trusted someone.

Recall when you were not disappointed.

Recall when you depended on someone.

Recall when you were forgotten, but then
remembered.

Recall when you needed something and got it.

Recall when you didn't get what you think
you needed, but got it elsewhere.

Recall when you possessed what someone
else wanted.

Recall when someone had what you wanted
and you were motivated.

Recall when you got what you wanted.

Recall when you didn't get what you
wanted but you tried again.

Recall when someone else got what you
wanted and you were happy for them.

Recall when you asked for something and
got what you wanted.

Recall when you asked again in a different
way to get what you wanted.

Recall when you negotiated a good deal for everyone.

Recall when you were physically carried.

Recall when you overcame being physically restrained.

Recall when you were encouraged.

Recall when you were trusted.

Recall when you were wanted.

Recall when someone liked you.

Recall when you made a friend.

Recall a time when you made up.

Recall when you were forgiven for some mistake.

Recall when you overcame a temptation.

Recall when you were sick and got better.

Recall when someone was happy to see you.

Recall when you were happy with yourself.

Recall when you didn't know what to do but eventually figured out what to do.

Recall when everything turned out okay.

Recall when you went somewhere new.

Recall when you went shopping and really liked what you got.

Recall when you got help solving a problem.

Recall when you cried and felt better.

Recall when you were embarrassed but everything turned out okay.

Recall when you kept a secret.

Recall when you made a mistake and learned a lesson.

Recall when you let go of feel unworthy.

Recall when you were discouraged but
  acted anyway.
Recall when others were late and it was
  okay.
Recall when you arrived somewhere on
  time.
Recall when you spoke up for yourself.
Recall when someone spoke up for you.
Recall when you were acknowledged.
Recall when you were needed and helped
  someone.
Recall when you were deceived and learned
  a lesson.
Recall when someone broke a promise and
  you eventually got what you needed.
Recall when you had a fun time in a group.
Recall when you were learning to drive.
Recall when you passed a driving test.
Recall finishing reading a book.
Recall visiting the library.
Recall watching TV late at night.
Recall getting up very early.
Recall making a deadline.
Recall a reunion.
Recall receiving a present.
Recall a party for you.
Recall falling but then getting back up.
Recall when you didn't miss out.
Recall learning something new about sex.
Recall being turned on.
Recall kissing someone.

Recall beginning something new.

Recall a loss that you eventually accepted.

Recall when someone died and you were grateful for the time you knew them.

Recall swimming with others.

Recall jumping off.

Recall an injury and being taken care of.

Recall being in a hospital.

Recall being driven somewhere.

Recall being fed.

Recall having a fun celebration.

Recall having a new look.

Recall traveling to a new place.

Recall completing a project.

Recall being rewarded.

Recall feeling robbed but getting what you needed.

Recall ending a fight.

Recall being considered.

Recall making a sacrifice for someone.

Recall making new friends.

Recall following your heart.

Recall giving up an addiction.

Recall avoiding a temptation.

Recall when you forgave yourself for a mistake.

Recall when you ate what you wanted.

Recall when you eventually found your way.

Recall when you had to be persistent.

Recall when you pushed yourself beyond your limits and felt proud.

Recall when you drove for hours and finally
    rested.
Recall when you stayed up all night.
Recall when you woke up feeling great.
Recall being helped in an emergency.
Recall being visited when sick.
Recall bringing flowers to someone.
Recall being late and it was okay.
Recall discovering things weren't as bad as
    you thought.
Recall making a wrong turn when things
    turned out okay.
Recall someone offering to help.
Recall thinking you were right but you were
    mistaken.
Recall learning an important lesson.
Recall expecting a reward.
Recall discovering that you were not
    cheated.
Recall anticipating being repaid.
Recall really looking forward to something.
Recall revealing an important wish.
Recall paying someone back.
Recall giving a gift without expecting any-
    thing in return.
Recall getting something for free.
Recall earning your way.
Recall buying something with your
    money.
Recall being asked to share.
Recall telling someone to wait.
Recall telling someone to watch out.

Recall defending yourself.

Recall winning an argument.

Recall teaching something.

Recall learning something for the first time.

Recall escaping from danger.

Recall taking a lesson.

Recall performing before others.

Recall making others laugh.

Recall speaking before a group.

Recall answering a question in a group.

Recall having the right answer.

Recall being picked.

Recall winning a game.

Recall being on the winning team.

Recall scoring a point.

Recall winning a prize.

Recall being happy for someone else.

Recall sharing something.

Recall waking up early to do something.

Recall being proud of yourself.

Recall when someone was proud of you.

Recall wanting to be noticed.

Recall when something was the perfect fit.

Recall being anxious and getting help.

Recall rushing to safety.

Recall not wanting to be noticed.

Recall making up for a mistake.

Recall when you were forgiven for being
    late.

Recall being remembered.

Recall introducing yourself.

Recall playing alone.

Recall playing with a friend.

Recall taking care of a sick animal.

Recall being happy to help.

Recall realizing why someone was mean to you.

Recall forgiving someone for being late.

Recall waiting for a long time but finally getting what you wanted.

Recall overcoming car trouble or running out of gas.

Recall someone apologizing to you.

Recall telling a secret.

Recall when you were asked to keep a secret.

Recall something you have always kept a secret.

Recall getting out of a tight situation.

Recall when you had to lie to protect someone.

Recall when you were free at long last.

Recall eventually doing well.

Recall when your prayers were finally answered.

Recall believing that the world was a magical place.

Recall trusting another with your secrets.

Recall meeting a stranger and liking him.

Recall becoming stronger.

Recall getting better at something.

Recall taking a risk and others appreciating you.

Recall being trusted.

Recall making the right decision.

Recall being surprised.

Recall when someone made you feel better.

Recall when someone believed in you.

Recall when you were not punished.

Recall when someone didn't interrupt you.

Recall saying everything that you felt.

Recall feeling really understood.

Recall smiling for a picture.

Recall being really excited about something.

Recall an injustice that was corrected.

Recall when you were protected.

Recall changing someone's mind.

Recall changing your mind.

Recall changing an opinion about someone.

Recall outgrowing something.

Recall leaving an unsupportive relationship.

Recall saying no and still being loved.

Recall having a different opinion and being liked.

Recall planning something really nice for someone.

Recall planning a party.

Recall seeing yourself in a picture.

Recall posing for a picture.

Recall being made to do something for your own good.

Recall being outraged by an injustice.

Recall hiring someone to do a job for you.

Recall delegating a responsibility.
Recall doing what you were supposed to do.
Recall disagreeing with someone you liked.
Recall being confident.
Recall feeling your father's love.
Recall feeling your mother's love.
Recall spending private time with your
    mother.
Recall spending private time with your
    father.
Recall being consoled by your mother.
Recall being consoled by your father.
Recall your father helping you.
Recall your mother helping you.
Recall being carried by your father.
Recall being held by your mother.
Recall being served by your father.
Recall being served by your mother.
Recall being told a story.
Recall wanting to please your mother.
Recall wanting to please your father.
Recall feeling your mother's approval.
Recall feeling your father's approval.
Recall feeling free to wander.
Recall having a secret hiding place.
Recall getting a lot of attention.
Recall winning a battle.
Recall traveling together in a group.
Recall cleaning up something.
Recall finishing a project.
Recall your father forgiving you.
Recall your mother forgiving you.

Recall your father protecting you.
Recall your mother protecting you.
Recall something your father taught you.
Recall something your mother taught you.
Recall your favorite breakfast food.
Recall your father taking care of you.
Recall your mother taking care of you.
Recall a sibling taking care of you.
Recall being lost but then found.
Recall when you were really happy to see
    someone.
Recall being invited to something.
Recall feeling special.
Recall feeling that you were different in a
    good way.
Recall saying no.
Recall being angry and powerful.
Recall being sad but not unhappy.
Recall being afraid but also confident.
Recall feeling sorry but not bad.
Recall feeling powerless but having faith.
Recall surviving an accident.
Recall hearing good news.
Recall saying good-bye to someone with
    love.
Recall starting over and finding love again.

Whenever you experience pain in the present, you will get additional support by exploring your past positive experiences. If the pain you feel in the present is linked to the past, any unresolved negative feelings will have a chance to come up when you ask these positive questions. By taking time to link your present pain with the pain of your past, you will be able to find immediate relief and heal your heart. Feel free to use this list again and again.

13

ALWAYS REMEMBER
THE LOVE

The most important element in starting over is always to remember the love. When we deliberately take time to remember the special moments we shared with a partner, we can most effectively heal our hearts. Eventually, we will be able to remember the love and not feel the pain. If we don't remember the love, then a big part of our hearts will remain closed for the rest of our lives.

Although at first this process of remembering the love may make us cry, these tears are healing tears and they will eventually make us feel better.

It is usually easier for us to remember the love when our partner is deceased or we are hoping to get back together. After a painful breakup or divorce, we may be so upset or angry with our ex that we don't want to remember the love. There is a way around this obstacle.

After a painful breakup we
may be so upset that we don't
want to remember the love.

If you are upset with your ex-partner, imagine that he or she has died. Recognize that the person you thought your partner is dead. If you are happy to be rid of him, go back and remember the person you thought he was and imagine that person has died. In this way, you are able once again to feel the part of you that can love.

On the other hand, if you are living in hope of getting back together, this can block your feelings of loss. If you are living in hope, it is important to give up hope temporarily. If reconciliation really is possible, you will be better prepared by having healed your heart.

You can't grieve a loss when you are
hoping to get back together.

With this preparation to connect with your love, you are ready to experience these healing visualizations. Wait until you have time to relax to do the exercises. Select one visualization to experience each week for the first twelve weeks of healing. Each day for a week, repeat the process; then move on to the next week's visualization.

Read the visualization slowly. After each question take at least ten seconds to reflect on your inner responses before moving on to the next question. Although it takes just a few moments to read an exercise, to do one requires at least ten minutes. After doing all twelve, you can go back and repeat your favorite ones.

You might want to put on some music in the background and read them or you may read them into a recorder with music and then lie back and let yourself go. This is a warm and comforting way to fall asleep at night. If you wish, you can order a recording of these visualizations that I have recorded over a background of soothing, heartfelt music. Call 1–888–627–7836.

VISUALIZATIONS FOR REMEMBERING THE LOVE

Before each visualization, take some time to relax your body. Be aware of the different parts of your body and just let go. Imagine you can breathe deeply into each part and just relax on the exhale. When your whole body is relaxed, then begin exploring your responses to these questions. When you have completed the visualization, bring yourself back to present time by repeating the above relaxation process. To ground yourself in present time, repeat the following phrase about ten times, completing the sentence each time. "Right now in my life I am in the process of _____."

For example, you might say:

"Right now I am in the process of healing
   my heart."
"Right now I am in the process of feeling
   better about myself."
"Right now I am in the process of moving
   on to find love again."
"Right now I am in the process of forgiving
   my ex-partner."
"Right now I am in the process of getting
   ready to meet the day."

WEEK 1

How You Met

Remember when you first met. How did you
meet? Where did you go? When did you first
feel romantic feelings? What did you want to
say but didn't? What did you say? What did
he/she say? What did you do? What did he/she
do? What was most unique or special about
him/her? Imagine you can go back in time and
look into his/her eyes. Feel the love in your
heart for him/her. How did he/she make you
feel? How else does he/she make you feel? As
you explore your feelings, focus on the love. As
you continue to look in his/her eyes, also feel
the pain of losing him/her. Feel how much you
miss that person.

As this pain comes up also focus on the love
you feel for him/her. Focus on the love. Love feels
good, love is expansive. Love is open and accept-

ing. This love you feel is healing the pain of your loss. One day soon your pain will go and only the love will remain.

WEEK 2

Your First Date

Remember your first romantic date. What did you do together? Remember your first touch? Remember being touched? Remember your first kiss? Remember realizing that you loved him/her and that you wanted to spend the rest of your life with him/her. Go back in time and remember how it felt to hold each other.

Grieve the loss of his/her presence as you remember lying so close to him/her. Feel the innocence of your connection. Feel your hopes and wishes. Feel the part of you that wanted to be all that you could be. Feel the part of you that wanted to make him/her happy. Remember hoping or believing that everything would work and you would live happily ever after.

Imagine cuddling up next to him/her. Feel your special bond and the warmth of your closeness. As your pain of missing him/her comes up, keep focusing on your love and closeness. Focus on the love. Love makes you feel safe and comforted. Love is warm and soothing. Love sets you free to be you and all that you want to be. One day soon your pain will go and only the love will remain.

WEEK 3

A Passionate Moment

Remember a passionate and intimate moment, a moment charged with the special love you shared. Remember the buildup. Remember your feelings of anticipation. What was involved in setting up this special occasion? Remember your excitement as the encounter progressed, what happened and where you were. Remember the temperature. Remember the smells in the air.

Breathe in and imagine you are there. Feel the passion you felt in your heart and body. Remember your own burning desire. Feel your partner's longing for you and his/her embracing you. Feel your desire to merge to be one. Feel the passion of your surrender as you both rise to the highest peaks of pleasure. At a delicious moment of union, you lie in each other's arms feeling peace and contentment.

And now, in present time, feel the emptiness in your heart, the desperate longing to feel once again that special connection with his/her body and soul. Feel the pain of separation while remembering the ecstasy of the special love that you shared. Let the pain you feel be mixed with the ecstasy of the love you shared. Feel that love and let it heal your soul. Love is peaceful, love is content. Find peace in the memories of your love. One day soon, the pain will be gone and you will be left with the quiet peace of your love.

WEEK 4

Feeling Supported

Remember a time when you felt your partner was really there for you. You needed him/her and he/she was so supportive. Recall what happened. What did you need? What did you say? What did he/she say? What did he/she do? What else did he/she do for you?

As you take a deep breath, imagine you are back in time. Imagine you are feeling those same needs. Feel your need for love, closeness, acceptance, trust, and caring. Feel how good it felt to belong, to be part of a loving relationship. Feel your gratitude for his/her support. Feel the joy of sharing your life with another. Feel the relief of not having to bear the burden of your life alone.

Let your heart be filled with gratitude. As you feel the burden and pressures of being alone, continue to focus on your gratitude. Thank him/her again for what he/she did. In your heart, acknowledge what you are grateful for. Feel the pain of the loss, but also feel the gratitude for all that he/she gave to you. One day soon your pain will be gone. Your life will once again be full with an abundance of love and support.

WEEK 5

The Simple Things

Remember the simple things that your partner used to do. Things like planning, organizing, shopping, cooking, driving, carrying a box, paying a bill, or mailing a letter. What are some of the little things he/she did for you? What else? What were some of his/her unique or weird behaviors? Things that no one did but him/her. Maybe it was the way he/she sneezed or the way he/she pronounced some word. Remember the way he/she looked. And remember the way he/she looked at you.

Take a deep breath and imagine you are back with him/her at a happy moment. Feel your warm affection for him/her and your appreciation for his/her caring. It feels so good when someone cares about us. When we are not alone. That to someone we are special.

Feel your special love as you feel the pain of being alone today. Let your soul be comforted by the memories of your special love. As you feel your pain, focus on the love. Feel your partner's love envelop and surround you. Imagine yourself wrapped in the softness of his/her love. Love is unbounded and eternal. Let him/her know that he/she is not forgotten and that you will always love him/her. One day soon your pain will go and you will continue to feel your special love.

WEEK 6

Sharing Good Fortune

Remember rejoicing in your partner's happiness. Recall a time when you were happy that your partner was happy. What happened to make him/her happy? How did you help him/her? Recall the joy of sharing his/her good fortune. Remember the first time you were able to please him/her. Remember how good it made you feel to make a difference in his/her life, how purposeful you felt caring so much for another.

Remember a time when you were successful and he/she was proud of you. He/she was genuinely happy for you. He/ she wanted you to succeed. Your happiness made him/her happy. How did it feel to share so freely your success with someone you love? Recall other times you shared good times together. What happened? What made the two of you happy?

As you remember his/her loving support, let it soothe the pain of emptiness. As you feel gratitude for his/her support, let it soothe your soul and help you endure the pain of your aloneness. Let his/her love comfort and help you to reach out once again for love and support. Thank him/her for affirming that you deserve to be loved, and with that support, resolve to get the support you need at this most important time in your life. One day soon your pain will be gone and you will share your heart once again.

WEEK 7

The Power of Love

Remember a time when you were sad or disappointed. What happened? What didn't happen that you wanted to happen? Remember how his/her love and support made your pain bearable. Remember the relief that you could let down your guard and share your vulnerable side. Remember the ease and comfort his/her love provided.

Take a deep breath and imagine you are back in time. Imagine him/her reaching over and giving you a hug. Feel your partner's gentle acceptance and understanding of who you are. Feel the freedom to share your sadness. Feel the relief of not having to carry your burdens alone.

Comforted by his/her loving support, feel the sadness of your loss today. Feel the longing in your heart to be with him/her and let his/her love comfort your sadness as it did before. Feel the power of your partner's acceptance and understanding and let that love make you whole again. Don't run away from love. Take the time you need and get the support you deserve. One day soon your pain will be gone and you will feel the full power of love once more in your life.

WEEK 8

Being Vulnerable

Remember a time when you were unsure or afraid and your partner believed in you. What were you afraid of? What could have happened that you didn't want to happen? How did it make you feel? Remember his/her support at that time when you were really vulnerable and he/she was there for you. Remember when he/she was there to say "I know you can do it. I believe in you." Or "Everything will be okay."

Take a deep breath and imagine yourself back in time. Feel the strength his/her love provided you at your most vulnerable moments. Feel the part of you that needed someone to reassure you and encourage you. Feel the deep appreciation you felt in response to his/her loving support.

Remembering his/her support, feel the vulnerability you feel without his/her support. Feel your fears that no one will love you or that you will never love again. Feel the fear that the sun will not shine again in your life. As you feel your fears, remember the strength that his/her support once gave you.

Appreciate that strength now by resolving to take the time you need to heal this loss. Don't hide your love away, let it out. Let others be there for you in your time of need. Make a promise to remember this strength and to feel that support as you begin this new chapter in your life. Honor your partner by taking his/her gifts and continuing to use them. Let him/her know that his love and support is not forgotten and will not be forgotten. One day soon, your pain will be gone and you will feel once more your strength and greatness.

WEEK 9

The Magic of Forgiveness

Remember a time when you made a mistake and your partner was forgiving of you. What happened? What was your mistake? How did you hurt him/her or disappoint him/her? How did his/her unconditional love, understanding, and acceptance make you feel?

Now, take a deep breath and imagine yourself back at that time.

Feel your sincere regret for hurting him/her. What did you not say that you would like to say now? Feel your loving remorse that says, "I love you, I am sorry for what happened." Feel the healing power of his/her unconditional love for you.

As you feel his/her loving support, feel the pain of your sorrow that there is nothing you can do to bring your partner back. As you feel the pain of your grief, feel the soothing influence of his/her love and forgiveness. Feel him/her forgiving you. Feel him/her saying, "I know you loved me. You did your best and that's all anyone could ask for." Feel the gift of his/her love.

Imagine your soul being bathed in the light of his/her love and forgiveness. Feel the innocence of your soul, bursting forth, like a flower open to the rays of your partner's love. As you feel this renewal, feel gratitude for the healing power of love. Know that soon your pain will be gone and you will freely love once more.

WEEK 10

Being Understood

Remember a time when you felt really understood. What happened? What did your partner say or do? Recall another time when others opposed you, but your partner stood by your side. Remember how it felt to be supported. Remember how it felt knowing that your partner understood the struggle you were having to deal with.

Take a deep breath and imagine you are back at that time. Remember how it felt to feel that he/she really understood what you were going through. He/she appreciated your efforts to do the right thing. He/she knew the whole story and he/she knew your pain. Breathe in a sigh of relief as you remember feeling his/her compassionate and understanding support.

Part of the pain of losing someone is the feeling that no one understands what we are going through. We feel no one could understand. As you feel this pain, remember the support you felt when your partner was there. Feel the comfort and ease that comes when someone knows us, when someone sees us and recognizes us with appreciation for our efforts, trials, tribulations, and achievements.

Remember the sweet nectar of your partner's understanding, which can only come when two souls come together in love and share many experiences and dreams together. Feel the aching hurt of your aloneness and let your soul be soothed by remembering the comfort you felt sharing your life and your many experiences with your partner. Reach out to others in pain and give your understanding. Recognize that they too can understand the depths of grief you are going through. One day soon, your pain will be gone and you will not be alone.

WEEK 11

Being Needed

Remember a time when you felt really needed. You belonged. You were a part of his/her life and he/she was a part of yours. Recall his/her reaching out to you for support and your being able to provide for him/her in some way.

Take a deep breath and go back in time. Remember how his/her love made you feel. Feel the joy of his/her appreciation for what you brought into his/her life. Feel the meaning he/she gave your life. Feel your connection to him/her. To lose him/her is like losing a limb. A part of you. An integral part of your life. A special and cherished part that can never be released.

As you grieve this loss, feel your sadness and sorrow, but also feel your gratitude for his/her gifts; feel grateful for all the special memories. Remember his/her needing and depending on your love. In your heart, let him/her know that he/she will never be forgotten.

Feel the bittersweet joy that comes from knowing that he/she will always be a part of you. You can always remember him/her and feel his/her special love. Know that as time passes it will be less painful to remember. The love in your heart for him/her will heal your wounds. With this love, you will be renewed and your life will be filled with the fullness of love.

WEEK 12

The Gifts of Love

Remember the gifts of love your partner brought into your life. Recall how they affected you. Recall how they made your life better. Recall what your life was like before he/she came along. How did he/she brighten up your life? How did he/she give you strength when you needed it? Recall when you both were happy together. Recall when you had fun together. Recall your partner giving you exactly what you wanted. Remember thanking God for the gift of your partner's love.

Take a deep breath and go back and imagine once again the joy of being in his/her presence. Bask in the sunshine of his/her love. Feel the sweetness of your love for him/her. Feel how happy you are to return for a few brief moments to your life before he/she left.

As you feel the pain of your loss, be comforted by remembering the joy your partner brought you. Let the loving memory of your partner wash away your pain. Your partner was an answer to your prayers, not just blind luck. God loves you and God has not deserted you.

Although you can't imagine it now, you will grow stronger from this and be able to give and receive more love than ever before. You have not been forgotten. You are still loved and you will love again. One day soon, the pain will be gone and you will fully experience God's love and grace once more.

14

---

101 WAYS TO HEAL OUR HEARTS

There are many different ways and processes for remembering our partner with love to assist us in healing our hearts. Anything that will help us experience our emotions of loss will assist us in the process. One path is not better than another, as long as it leads us back to love, understanding, forgiveness, gratitude, and trust.

These are 101 ways to remember and honor your loved one. Instead of feeling powerless to do anything to feel better, use these suggestions to do something each day to nurture the natural healing process. Use any of these suggestions to assist you in remembering your partner with love to stay in touch with your feelings.

This list can also be used for letting go of a relationship that ended in divorce, separation, or breakup. If we are heartbroken and our partner is still alive, then for the sake of healing our hearts we need to recognize that the person he was or we thought he was is gone. It is as if he had died.

Using this perspective you can properly grieve your loss.

1. Listen again and again to songs or music that touch your soul.
2. Go to movies or watch videos that make you cry.
3. Read one of your favorite kinds of books or join a book club to discuss a book.
4. Go on an adventure, even if it is just for a day. Take time to create a new experience for yourself, to experience yourself in a new way.
5. Go dancing or do something fun. Grieving doesn't mean being down all the time. We need time to do things that will also lift our spirits by being around others who are having a good time. It is okay if this brings up more sadness.
6. Drive around to the places where you spent special times with your partner or return to the place where you first met.
7. Read old letters to and from your partner.
8. Imagine the presence of your partner in front of you and pour out all your feelings, believing or imagining that he can hear you and respond to you. This can also be done by asking a friend to sit in front of you and role-play being your partner. All your friend has to do is to hold your hands and to listen.
9. Watch home videos of your time together.
10. Continue to burn a long-burning candle in

her memory or burn scented candles to remind you of the sweetness of your love.

11. Look over your photo album alone and then with friends. Pick a different friend each time and it will enrich the experience. Tell stories of old times together.

12. Put together a book of his life for family and friends.

13. Keep certain of her personal effects around you.

14. Keep his picture up near your bed. Say good night and good morning to his picture.

15. Tell your story of the loss or breakup to all your friends one by one. Each time you tell it, you will be healing a new layer of pain and opening up to more love.

16. Join a support group to tell your story. Listen to others share their stories of love. Hearing their pain will assist you in feeling your own. Each week share your experiences of gradually getting better.

17. Take a healing workshop to surround yourself with others who are sharing a similar experience. The process of healing is always easier with the support of a group.

18. Go on some kind of group activity or vacation. Sharing with others in some new experience will help nurture the new you.

19. Make a list of all your partner's good qualities and share it with your friends, again one at a time.

20. Participate in chat rooms on the Internet.

Being anonymous can be very liberating. You can test your new wings out. Try being totally honest and experiencing a new freedom.

21. Learn something new in honor of your partner. Take a class in something new or something that your partner was interested in.

22. Buy a gift for yourself and imagine that it is a gift from your partner. Think of what he would want you to have to comfort you in your grief and then get it for yourself.

23. Remember some behavior that you do simply because your partner liked it and then continue doing it to remember her.

24. Put flowers on her grave or in front of her picture, every day for a week, once a week for three months, and once a month for the next year. Then once a year, on her birthday, for the rest of your life.

25. Make a list of how he contributed to your life and the lives of others. Ask others this question as well.

26. Express your feelings of gratitude to her in a letter.

27. Write a letter from him encouraging you and mail it to yourself.

28. Dedicate a special part of the garden to him/her.

29. Buy something beautiful to put on your mantel at this time to remind you of her.

30. Write a forgiveness letter, forgiving him/her for every mistake that you can remember,

have a friend or therapist role play him/her while you read your letter. As you read your letter, imagine your partner is listening.

31. Write an apology letter, acknowledging every mistake you think you made. Role-play this with a therapist or friend.

32. Write a letter from her forgiving you for your mistakes and mail it so you receive it later. Role-play this with a therapist or friend. Close your eyes and imagine as your therapist reads the letter that your partner is speaking.

33. Write an apology letter from him/her to you and mail to yourself. Role-play this as well. Have the therapist read the apologies. With your eyes closed, express your forgiveness and any other feelings.

34. Think of a charity your partner cared about or believed in and make a donation in her name, particularly if there is some public recognition associated with it, like a little plaque of some kind.

35. Create a special time one hour a day to do healing exercises or listen to healing-the-heart tapes and do visualization exercises. Pick a special music to play each time you grieve your loss.

36. Tell your friends that grieving makes you feel better. Although it is painful, it feels good to feel our love for our partner. Otherwise, your friends will become impatient with you for taking so long to grieve a loss.

If they haven't been through it, they just can't understand.

37. Take time to hear the stories of others who have lost love. By putting yourself in their shoes you experience that you are not alone. Your loneliness becomes less.

38. Go somewhere new and meet some new people. New experiences always bring out something new within ourselves.

39. Get a new pet to take care of. Caring for a pet can soothe and heal your heart. It will also make you feel young.

40. Reach out and ask for the support of your friends. They will gladly give it. Ask them to invite you for dinner. If they seem to be avoiding you, it is only because they don't know what to say or how to behave. They would love to know what they can do for you.

41. Don't rush the healing process. Plan to be in the grieving process for three to nine months. You pick the number. If you don't plan it then you may avoid this special time of healing. You will rush by this special window of opportunity to heal your heart. This will be the most special memory of your life.

42. Center yourself in the present using this ritual each morning when you wake up: Look in the mirror and say aloud, "Right now in my life, I am in the process of . . ." Complete the sentence each time with the next thought that comes to mind. Repeat this ten times.

43. Imagine something special you would be doing this week if your partner was still with you and then do that.

44. Imagine how you would feel if you fully believed that what happened was perfect.

45. Count your blessings. Often, when we are grieving a loss, we forget to appreciate what we do have.

46. Be patient with yourself. Instead of getting frustrated when you experience a setback, reward yourself with a treat.

47. If you become depressed, rent ten funny videos and watch them in one day.

48. Ask your friends for a hug. When we have lost a source of affection in our lives, we can still get the touch we need by asking for hugs. Simply say, "Would you give me a hug?"

49. Get a massage every week. Physical touch is just as important as love. To heal our hearts we must also take care of our bodies.

50. Give yourself permission to feel that life isn't fair. Reflect on the dreams and goals that you had hoped to share together. Feel your disappointment and write a letter expressing your feelings.

51. Don't try to be "up" and in a good mood for your friends. Give yourself permission to hit bottom. It is only by accepting the waves of grief that you will heal your heart. By respecting the healing process, the pain will go away completely and permanently.

52. If you were in Jerusalem you could visit the

Wailing Wall to experience other people in grief; a modern equivalent is going to a workshop on healing the past or on grieving the loss of a loved one.

53. If you didn't get to say good-bye the way you wished, then sitting with a friend or therapist, close your eyes, hold hands facing each other with eyes closed, and imagine having an opportunity to say good-bye. Role-play the situation exactly the way you would want it. Switch roles and imagine what your partner would say as well.

54. If you feel guilty about the loss because you feel that you could have done something, share this notion with a friend or therapist. To help find self-forgiveness, make it up. Commit yourself to doing something good for someone in need. Give of yourself the way you wish you had given to them. Make a gift of love and support to someone in need. Giving of ourselves always helps us to let go of guilt or shame.

55. Connect back to the earth. Go for a walk in the morning. If weather permits, walk barefoot on the grass. Breathe deeply the fresh air of the early morning.

56. If you feel a need to get away to heal yourself, take early vacation leave from your job as soon as possible. They will understand your situation.

57. Cut out his/her obituary in the paper and read it every few days.

58. Have a friend videotape or record the funeral service and reception afterwards to replay later when you really need that comfort. Sometimes we are still in shock when the funeral occurs. It can be days after the funeral before our pain comes up, and that is when we really need the support the most. Have your friend with the video camera or tape recorder ask others to say the things that they loved about your partner. Have them each tell a little story of how they met your partner and what kind of person they thought he or she was. Then at times watch the video or listen to the tape.

59. Repeat to yourself, "I will get through this." Remember other people have been through this. Soon the pain will be gone.

60. Remember when you first met; write a letter of gratitude to the person who introduced you and send it.

61. Write a letter to the complaint department of the universe. Vent all your feelings of anger, resentment, and hurt. Then explore the other levels of feelings like sadness, fear, and sorrow. Write a response letter from God or an angel and mail it to yourself.

62. Ask a friend to come over to just hang out. Let him/her know that he/she doesn't have to say anything. Practice just being together with no talking or doing anything. No TV, no cooking, no reading. Just go for a walk or sit for an hour looking at the sunset or the

moonrise. The peace you feel will comfort your soul.

63. Give yourself permission to be like a child. If your loss brings up unresolved issues of the past, go to the zoo or a fun theme park with a friend or family member. Be around children who are having fun.

64. Go to weddings. Surrounding yourself with love is the best cure. It will bring up grief, but it will be healing.

65. If you enjoy competitive sports, don't hold back. Keep competing. In particular, sports can help a man get in touch with his feelings of aliveness and desire.

66. Go to church and pray to God. In your heart, share your deepest feelings of inadequacy. Feel God's grace surrounding you and carrying you during this dark night of your soul.

67. Put yourself first. This is your time to be pampered. Release any obligations that are making your life crazy. You are grieving a loss and have other things that you have to do right now.

68. If your friends don't ask you about your feelings, let them know what you need. Tell them, "I am feeling a lot of grief and I just need to feel sorry for myself for ten minutes. All you have to do is listen and I will feel better. I just need to get it out." Once they have agreed, then talk about times you remember with your partner and let your sadness come up as you speak.

69. Don't hold back your tears. It is okay to cry. Some may need to be alone to cry. That is okay, too. Crying is good for the soul. For a really good cry listen to the music of the Broadway play *Les Misérables*. Better yet, go to see it and then listen to the album over and over.

70. Be careful to minimize conflict and avoid fights regarding the division of property. If a family member fights, try to remember that what he is really upset about is the loss. In handling the settlement after a divorce, have a long separation so you have done most of your healing before the actual divorce settlement is decided on.

71. When you are in pain, don't keep it a secret. This is the time to reach out and bare your soul.

72. After a death or divorce, don't tell your children they have to be strong. Don't share all your grief with your children; instead, be there for them as much as possible. Handle most of your grief while they are in school or you are away from them. Don't look to your children for solace. Doing so will prevent them from looking to you for solace.

73. Don't make it worse than it is. Just as it is wrong to encourage your children not to grieve, it is also important not to make it a bigger loss than they experience it to be. It may be a while before they are able to deal with their feelings. They may become very

upset about other things. The best approach is to listen. Ask the question, "What else is bothering you?" again and again.

74. When you see others in love and begin to feel sorry for yourself, do an anger process. While looking in the mirror, express what you are angry about for a couple of minutes, then express what you want for a few minutes, and then affirm out loud what you deserve for a few minutes. You will feel better immediately.

75. When your ex-partner is praised and you become envious or angry, take some time to write out a list of your secret fears. Fears like "I will never be loved again" or "I am not good." Then finish the exercise with expressing what you feel grateful for.

76. Do some community service, particularly around people who will appreciate what you have to offer.

77. Ask yourself how you would feel if you knew for sure that in two years your life would be filled with love and you would be happy again. Then visualize this with your eyes closed. Imagine yourself in the future and describe out loud to a friend or therapist how you feel. Use these phrases to draw out your positive feelings: "I feel grateful for . . ." "I feel happy because . . ." "I am confident that . . ."

78. Drive to the top of a mountain, to a river, or to the sea and create a little ritual of saying

good-bye. Make it a half day's journey or walk. Much of the healing takes place on the journey. Scatter flowers in all directions as an offering and expression of your love.

79. Talk to a religious leader, priest, pastor, rabbi, or other spiritual guide to get spiritual support and guidance.

80. Think of something your partner would have wanted to do or left incomplete and do it.

81. Call up his friends and let them know all the details surrounding his death. If you are grieving a divorce, take time to share with your friends how you tried to make it work, but realized that you were not right for each other. Try saying good things about how hard your partner tried even if a part of you doesn't yet believe it.

82. Always seek to forgive. The easiest way to forgive is demonstrated by Christ while he was on the cross. He said, "Father, forgive them, for they know not what they do." We can most easily forgive when we recognize that our partner really didn't know what he was doing.

83. Recognize that the pain you feel today will prepare you to be there for others in the future. By healing your pain you will develop an incredible compassion and love for others when they go through pain. You will learn valuable lessons that you can pass on to others.

84. Reflect on what you need when you are in

pain so that you will know how much you are needed when others are in pain. Just being with someone in pain without talking can be very comforting. In our darkest hours, we just need to feel a loving presence nearby.

85. Resolve to be the best person you can. Often when we feel and release some of our pain, we are inspired. In that inspired moment, make a list of the qualities that you want to embody in your life.

86. Keep a journal of the first thirty days of your healing journey. Record some of your thoughts, feelings, and experiences from each day.

87. Write a poem or read a book of poems.

88. Turn to God for solace. It is sometimes in our darkest moments when we best can humble ourselves before God. Take this time to reevaluate or update your spiritual beliefs.

89. Don't limit your grieving time each day. Everyone is different and every day will be different. Be flexible and take as long as you want.

90. Ride the waves of feeling. Don't expect to be down all the time or up all the time. It is not a betrayal of your partner to have moments of joy and relief. Our grief is not the declaration of our love, it is the process of letting go of our pain. With each release we may feel incredibly joyful and high.

91. Find your own unique way of grieving. Some people are very dramatic and others

are more restrained. If you are dramatic, make sure there are times when you are also giving thanks and feeling good. If you are more restrained, make sure that you don't suppress the pain inside.

92. Don't expect others to know your needs. Often we are embarrassed to ask for support. Let friends and relatives know and keep asking.

93. Visit the maternity ward at a hospital. After a loss, it is good to connect with the joyous and loving energy surrounding birth. In a way, you are being reborn to a new life as well.

94. Remember that the dawn of a new day comes after the darkest moment of the night. Things may get darker, but the light of love and relief will come.

95. Keep active for a part of each day, using your body in a way that makes you breathe deep. Breathing and movement are very important to stimulate the lymph system, which purifies the body during a healing crisis.

96. Plant a tree or a special plant in your partner's honor and nurture its growth.

97. Buy a special piece of jewelry to wear to always remember the beauty of your love.

98. Wear a black string around your wrist to acknowledge that you are in the grieving process.

99. Each day write down in your journal three memories from your relationship.

100. Make a list of all the things you will never do together that you wish you could have. In grieving this loss, you will eventually be able to appreciate fully the time you did share and then be ready to move on.

101. When you are feeling pain, take time to process the four healing emotions by linking your pain with the past, reliving it, and enriching the experience. Practice the feeling better exercise to heal your pain.

By deliberately staying in touch with your love and feelings during this critical time of healing your heart, it will truly become a time of greatness for you, although it might be hard to believe all this will pass. You will rise again to experience life once more in all its glory. Think of this time as getting through a cold winter. Use these different processes and techniques to make sure you stay protected, healthy, and warm. Although it may be a long season, remember that soon the coldness will leave and the freshness and warmth of springtime is just around the corner.

PART TWO

Starting Over on Venus

Starting over on Venus is often different from starting over on Mars. Men and women face very different challenges. What is good for a man may not be good for a woman. What she experiences as an obstacle may not be an obstacle for him. It is easier to decide the right course of action when we take our differences into consideration.

When we are in pain, it is not always wise to follow our instincts. What feels like the right thing to do may not always be the best choice. After a loss, we are suddenly faced with a new life and many choices. It is hard to know what to do. What we decide may affect us for the rest of our lives. Without a complete understanding of the healing journey, men and women may unknowingly push away opportunities to find true and lasting love.

In part two, we will explore twenty-three common challenges women face when starting over. Then, in part three, we will explore twenty-three common challenges men face. The insights into the dynamics of starting over that you will find here will support you in finding love again. Although these two parts are devoted to the separate issues of Mars and Venus, there is always some overlap. Men and women will benefit from reading each of the sections.

With an awareness of the possible mistakes as you face this important fork in the road, you will be more skillful in avoiding unnecessary pain. This important preparation will ready you to take the risk to love again. By rising to the occasion of healing your heart and then finding love again, you will be moving on to express your highest potential for success and happiness in life.

1

CARRYING A
BIG LIST

A woman commonly protects herself by carrying a list of requirements. Before opening up to a man, she will test him. He must satisfy her list of conditions and requirements before she is willing to get involved. Unfortunately, if her feelings are still unresolved, that list will be too long. Instead of opening up to the possibility of a loving relationship, she will reject it. She will remain safe but alone.

When we are still hurting from a loss, our tendency to protect ourselves is naturally greater. We are, appropriately, overprotective. As we have already explored, when a wound is healing it needs special protection. After it has healed, we naturally go back to normal protections. If we do not heal a wound, we may be overprotective for the rest of our lives.

While we are healing, we are,
appropriately, overprotective.

When a woman is overprotective, her list tends to get longer and longer. To protect herself from getting hurt again, she becomes excessively critical, judgmental, or demanding of a potential relationship. In simple terms, she becomes too picky. No man will ever be good enough. No matter how hard she tries to be open and receptive, she will reject what she can have and she will want what she cannot have. In her mind, all the good men have already been taken. These are some examples of the way she may test or judge a man:

HOW WOMEN MAY TEST AND JUDGE MEN

1. He was married before; I wonder what went wrong. He doesn't talk much about her. Why did that marriage end? He is hiding something. . . .

2. I wonder if he will call me when he says he will. If he doesn't, then I don't think I can trust him. . . .

3. I'll bet he just wants to have sex, and he is not interested in having a real relationship.

4. Let's see if he picks me up on time. I'm not getting involved again with a man who puts me at the bottom of the list. . . .

5. I don't think he will ever make a commitment. He has dated so many other women.

6. He is over thirty-five and not married. He's probably another man afraid of intimacy. I am not going to waste my time with him.

7. He lives in his head. He'll never open up to me. If I get involved, I want a man who can open up to me.

8. He is not very responsible; maybe he is one of these men who never grew up. I don't want to be his mother.

9. If he is not funny or entertaining, then I am out of here. I have been in relationships that were just too serious.

10. I don't like the way he dresses. If he doesn't care about himself, he will not be able to care about me.

11. He doesn't take care of his health the way I do. I need someone who thinks the way I do.

12. He watches a lot of sports. I want someone who will want to do the things I want to do. I don't want to be another sports widow.

13. He is not very neat or organized. I will probably have to clean up after him and keep his life organized. I have been through that; I don't want that responsibility again.

14. He is a very attractive and charming man. How would I ever be able to trust that he would be faithful? So many women would want him.

15. He is so involved in his work. There is no way I want to compete with that. His work would always be more important than me.

16. He is too involved with his kids. I would never get to feel special or adored.

17. He is too old to change. He is probably set in his ways. I don't want to get stuck with him.

18. He is obviously attracted to younger women. He would never be content to be with an older woman.

19. I wonder how much money he makes. If he cannot take care of himself, how could he take care of me? I want a man with some money. Maybe he wants me to take care of him.

20. We don't have enough in common. Unless we have enough shared interests, we cannot be right for each other.

21. What would my parents or friends think of him? I know they would think I was settling for less.

The need to judge or test a partner is not wrong. It is important to make sure a partner fulfills our unique needs and wishes. Every person has his own priorities. A woman's list of judgments and tests becomes a problem only when it prevents her from saying yes to going out on dates and giving love a chance. By getting to know many potential partners, she will discover that some of her concerns drop away and her need for perfection lessens. Eventually, she will be able to identify clearly the right man for her. Instead of looking for perfection, she will find the perfect man for her.

2

THE NEW PRESSURES
OF DATING

The tendency to reject potential sources of love is compounded by the new pressures of dating. Women today push away love because they feel an enormous pressure from society, and men, to become sexual right away in a relationship. If a woman wants to take time before getting intimate, she is labeled as old-fashioned or prudish. Everywhere we turn, we see fast women and fast sex. It is in the movies, on TV, on billboards, in advertisements, and in every magazine.

If a woman wants to take time
before getting intimate, she is labeled
as old-fashioned or prudish.

Although a woman should feel free to enjoy sex when she wants, she should not feel pressured. To the extent a woman succumbs to this pressure, her need to protect herself increases even more. In her mind, she reasons this way: If I am gong to have sex right away, then I must make sure the guy I go out with is someone I would want to have sex with. Instead of having the freedom to go out with a guy and eventually get to know him, she feels pressure to assess him right away. It is all or nothing.

This is a losing battle. Even if her heart is completely healed, it still takes time to get to know someone. It takes time to know if she wants to be intimate with a man. If she meets a man and doesn't know if she wants to be intimate, she will say no to protect herself from the obligation of having sex. Not only does he get rejected, but she doesn't give herself an appropriate opportunity to find love again. Who knows, after a delightful evening her feelings of doubt may go away.

Women approach sex very differently from men. A man can know right away if he wants to have sex with a woman. Women are the opposite. They need to take time. To experience the freedom to find love, a woman must first recognize that she doesn't have to be intimate right away. It is her choice. If she can comfortably say no to having sex right away, then she is free to date men without being so picky. She can then choose to have sex when she is ready.

3

DATE AROUND, BUT DON'T SLEEP AROUND

A woman pushes away love by associating dating with sex. To become free from her expectations of perfection and carrying a big list, the best solution is to throw it away temporarily. She should date around, but not sleep around. As long as she doesn't get serious with any one man, she doesn't need to protect herself from getting hurt. We only get hurt when we become attached to a person and then lose their love. If we remain unattached for a while, then we can experience love in many ways without getting hurt.

One healthy approach to avoid getting hurt while opening the heart is for a woman to date three men during the same time period. She should have one man on the way out, one man more current, and one new man on the way in. As long as she is not getting sexual or intimate with any of these men, there are no hurt feelings. In addition, by dating many men, she has an even stronger basis to refuse sex. She can easily say no to sex with a partner because she is also dating someone else. A man does not get his feelings hurt if she clearly lets him know that she is dating someone else as well.

Date one man on the way out,
one man more current, and
one new man on the way in.

Some women first resist this idea by saying, "Three men! I wish I could get one date!" These are actually the women who need to practice this the most. If a woman is not being asked out on dates, then some part of her is clearly pushing opportunities away. The reason she is not getting dates is because she is too picky. She is putting out the message in some way that she is not interested.

To start dating around, a woman
needs to throw away her list and
lower her standards.

To change this pattern, she needs to make a pledge to herself only to date men whom she would not want to marry and with whom she would definitely not want to have sex. Ideally, these are men that show an interest in her, but to whom she is not sexually attracted. This pledge will free her to begin going out on dates without feeling any pressures to become intimate. As she experiences the opportunities to give and receive friendship on a date, she will begin to open up her heart without having to protect herself. With the freedom to say no to sex, she will be able to say yes to sex at the right time for her.

It takes time to discover a person's good qualities. It is not fair or prudent to judge a book by its cover. By taking time to date around without the possibility of getting hurt, she is able to break free from her judgments and experience what a man truly has to offer her and how much she has to give. As long as she doesn't get too intimate, she can have a lot of fun while growing in her ability to trust love again.

Other women resist this idea because it doesn't feel natural. They say, "I can't date more than one man at a time. I am monogamous by nature." This may be true, but to date around does not mean to sleep around. We are so conditioned in our society to associate dating with sleeping together that it is hard to conceive of the possibility of dating without being sexually intimate. If a woman thinks she cannot date many men, it is only because she has not tried with this new perspective.

It is not uncommon to feel, "I can have only one *best* friend," but this does not exclude the possibility of having other friends. In a similar manner, dating around does not conflict with being monogamous. Be monogamous now with your soul mate who is yet to come. While waiting for your best friend to come along, have many other friends. Date around until you find someone very special and then stop dating the others. When you believe that you have found someone who may be your soul mate, then this is the time to have an exclusive relationship.

4

GLORIFYING
OUR PAST

Although it is most common for a woman to carry a big list when she has been hurt or mistreated by a man in her past, it can happen when a woman has been loved and nurtured as well. When a loved one is deceased, it is quite natural to glorify his good qualities to such a degree that no man can ever live up to his standard. Even if a relationship ends in divorce, a woman may still glorify certain good qualities of her ex-partner.

Men display this tendency to glorify the past as well. To the degree that we, both men and women, are still attached to a past partner, no future partner could ever compare. Until we have released our attachment, we are unable to appreciate all of what a new partner can offer us.

To the extent that we are still living in our past, we cannot fully appreciate the opportunities that exist in present time.

To overcome this tendency to compare, we need not fight it, but instead respect it. It is not possible to let go of our past right away. It takes time. When we begin dating, we just need to be aware of this. We should not expect someone to replace our partner or stand up to him in comparison. Instead, we need to recognize that over time this will change.

Although we will still compare in our minds, if we lower the stakes and just date to experience friendship and companionship and not to find a soul mate, we will not compare as much. We are more free to appreciate what we have. Certainly no new partner could be "better," he can be different. It is a limited belief to think that our hearts could be so small as to love only one person or to think that only one person could love us. As our heart is healed, there is plenty of room to love again.

It is a limited belief to think
only one person could love us.

The mistake men and women both make is to reject opportunities for relationship simply because a partner does not appear to measure up. It is too limiting to think, Well, this person does not make me feel the same way. Of course a new person cannot make us feel the same way, but over time that could change. The prudent course of action is to date around until we have completely let go. With new experiences of love and friendship to hold on to in present time, it is easier to let go of our past.

5

STAYING STUCK
IN GRIEF

Another way a woman commonly protects herself from getting hurt again is to remain stuck in her sadness and grief. Although it is lonesome, it is safer than confronting the possibility of getting involved again. When she holds on to her grief to avoid confronting her fears, the bittersweetness of grieving eventually turns to despair and hopelessness. Even though she may try to move on, mysteriously she remains gripped by her depression.

When a woman does not give herself permission to be angry or outraged by her loss, it can obstruct the healing process. To move beyond grief, she needs to feel her other emotions. For men and women, when anger is not fully felt and released it may easily cause us to stay stuck in sadness and the fear of moving on.

By first feeling and then letting go of
her anger, the resulting feelings of
entitlement, forgiveness, and gratitude
help to lessen her fears.

When single again after the death of a spouse,
it can be very difficult to feel angry. It is hard to
blame someone when his death was accidental or
the result of a terminal disease. On the other
hand, after a divorce or breakup, it may be easier
to feel anger but not as easy to let go with forgiveness and gratitude. In Chapter Twenty, we will
explore in greater detail how to overcome these
challenges.

6

THE BETRAYAL OF
LOVING AGAIN

Another way we push away love is not giving ourselves permission to love again. Particularly when a spouse is deceased, it may feel like a betrayal to start a relationship again. As the heart heals, it becomes clear that a spouse in heaven would never want his partner on earth to be deprived of love. All angels in heaven rejoice when we open our hearts to love. If we do not give ourselves permission to love, we may remain stuck in our grief. This pattern of holding on to grief is beautifully illustrated in the movie *Mrs. Brown*.

To love again, we must give ourselves permission to feel our positive feelings as well as our negative. We need to give ourselves permission to love again. These are three common limiting beliefs that need to be questioned and then released:

- **"I should not love again. My partner would feel betrayed and hurt."** To love again is never a betrayal of our partner. If she is deceased, she only wants us to be happy. She would want us to live in present time and move on in our lives. We can find love again and also hold a special love for our deceased partner. On the other side, there are no jealous feelings. If you died, would you want your partner to live out the rest of his life alone without love?

- **"If I am happy, then I did not really love my partner."** To be happy again does not mean that we did not love our deceased partner. Happiness arrives when we are in the process of getting what we want and need. Everyone needs love. To receive the gifts of love in present time does not in any way mean that we do not still love our past partner. It is okay to be happy again. It is not as if we are happy that our partner is gone. We are happy for other reasons. We are happy that we are in the process of getting what we need and deserve in life.

- **"If I am not grieving the loss then I don't really miss him."** We do not grieve a loss just because we loved someone. We grieve a loss because we are still attached. Through the grieving process, we are actually giving up our attachment. It does not mean in any way that we are giving up our love for the deceased. After we release our attachment, our partner still lives on in our hearts. When our hearts are healed, we are able to feel our love for our partner, but the pain and grief are gone.

Reflecting on our loss may still bring up some sadness, but it is infused with the joy of loving him, not the pain of missing him.

Sometimes it feels as if love hurts. It doesn't. When we love someone it feels great. We are our happiest when we are loving. Losing love is what hurts. When we lose someone we love, it hurts because we are resisting our loss, not because we love them. We are not yet accepting the reality that they are gone. Once we are able to accept our loss the pain goes away. Letting go of the pain does not mean that we have stopped loving our partner. It actually means the opposite. When our pain is healed, we are able to feel the sweetness of the love we felt before he died.

7

SEX AND
SELF-ESTEEM

Another common mistake women make while starting over is to sleep around in order to build up their self-esteem. A woman may seek a man's affection and attention to feel worthy of love, particularly if she was romantically neglected in her last relationship. It's hard to feel good about yourself when the person you live with ignores you or takes you for granted. It's even more difficult if you find out that he is in love or attracted to someone else. To feel special again, a woman is easily tempted to use her sexual favors as a way to win another man's attention and affection.

Unfortunately, this approach inevitably backfires. Looking outside herself for love, she is affirming that her worthiness is dependent on a man's affection and attention. Although it is healthy to depend on a man for romantic stimulation, it is not healthy to depend on him to feel worthy of such affection. Ideally, she must first feel worthy within herself and then get a man's affection. If she feels worthy of love only after getting it, she will be too dependent on him. Ultimately, this unhealthy neediness will turn him off and once again she will be hurt.

Ideally, a woman's sense of worthiness
should not come from a man's
attention and affection.

It is far better for her to focus on healing her heart without depending on a man's attention or affection. For men and women, the basis of having a healthy relationship is first loving ourselves and feeling worthy of love. Then we will attract and be attracted to someone who can love us the way we deserve. When our sense of worthiness comes from within, we are ready to depend on another for love and support. When we have a strong sense of who we are, we can bond with another without losing a healthy sense of our worth.

Taking time to process our unresolved feelings instead of dating has the effect of taking back our sense of self-worth. When we can feel angry instead of just sad for the ways we have been neglected in the past, we are automatically affirming our worthiness. When we can feel our anger and then release it with forgiveness, we are generally ready to start dating again. Taking time to heal our hearts is a much more powerful way to boost our self-esteem.

8

SEX, OBLIGATION, AND SELF-WORTH

Another way a woman pushes away love is by feeling obligated to have sex. Often a woman will refuse a man's gifts because she feels she will be obligated to return his favors with sex. Sometimes, when I suggest to a woman that she go on a date, allow a man to pay for her meal, but not have sex, her response is, "Why would a man want to take me out if I don't have sex with him? What is in it for him?" Sadly, this is a common response. It is a sign of diminished self-worth. She clearly doesn't recognize her worth to a man.

When a woman feels this way, it often implies that she feels obligated to satisfy a man's sexual urges simply because he took her out to dinner. A woman will refuse a man's offer to pay for dinner because she doesn't want him to feel she is obligated in any way. This kind of thinking reveals an epidemic of low self-esteem. A woman must learn to receive a man's gifts without feeling obligated to pay him back with sex.

There are many women who have very high self-worth, when it comes to work and business. When it comes to relationships, they fall back into thinking their only worth to a man is their sexual favors. A woman does not recognize that a man primarily cherishes the opportunity simply to be with her, to do nice things for her, and to experience the opportunity to make her happy. Sure, on the surface he may be looking for sex, but a little higher up he is looking for love just as she is.

Women fall back into thinking t
heir only worth to a man is
their sexual favors.

It is hard for a woman to know her worth. In history, women were valued primarily as home-makers. Today, times have changed. Just as a woman is no longer just looking for a bread-winner, a man is no longer just looking for a mother for his children. We are living in a time of changing values. Men and women are looking for love, romance, and passion.

A woman's new worth to a man is basically who she is and the love she has to share. He enjoys the many wonderful ways she may support him, but his real hunger is for her love. It is not just sex. As a relationship progresses, sex becomes a way for her to communicate her love to him, but certainly it is not the only way.

Sex is to men what marriage is to women. It is the highest reward of love. Thinking men just want sex is like saying that women just want to get married. Although there is some truth to these statements, they are too limiting. Men also want to get married, but that thought comes later. Likewise, women also want sex, but that desire is delayed.

When a man cares about a woman, though he may want to have sex, he also wants to just spend time with her. When a woman cares for a man, she may ultimately want to marry him, but she also just enjoys being with him. She is not pretending to be happy in order to get married. At the same time, she is not wrong for hoping they get married. In a similar manner, a man is not wrong hoping they have sex.

If they go out to dinner, he doesn't feel obligated to marry her. In a similar manner, a woman should not feel obligated to have sex just because he paid for her dinner. She owes him nothing but a smile and a thank-you. It is a big mistake for women to feel obligated to return a man's gift of love with sex.

A man doesn't feel obligated
to get married after going out on
a date; why should a woman
feel obligated to have sex?

If sex is not available, and a man cares for a woman, he will still want to take her out and share a nice time together. He is looking to give and receive affection not just because she will give him something later. He may be hoping for something later, but that is not the only motivation. By saying no to immediate sexual gratification, men and women get a chance to experience the real reason they are drawn together: the need to love.

Unfortunately for a man, if he doesn't get sex, then he may feel as if he is the only guy not getting it. Men not only feel the cultural pressure to have sex right away, but also his hormones pressure him as well. Women begin to feel a strong urge to have sex after about the age of thirty-seven. Of course she enjoys sex before that time, but around thirty-seven she may become like a young man wanting it all the time. Ironically, after about thirty-seven a man's sexual urge diminishes. While her testosterone levels are rising, his are beginning to drop off a little.

> While a man's testosterone levels are
> dropping, at age thirty-seven a
> woman's sexual urges are increasing.

Wherever a man looks, it appears as if everyone else is getting sex, so if he isn't, then why not? It is hard on his ego when a woman doesn't respond to his sexual hopes. At the same time, she is not responsible. He needs to find his self-worth without depending on a woman's sexual favors.

Yet how she rejects him can make things much easier for him. A clear message from her that she is already dating other men can make it much easier for him to take. He can easily understand that she doesn't want to hurt another person. If she is already seeing someone else, then he can save face. When this is the case, instead of feeling like a failure, if he cares enough he is then pleasantly challenged to be the one for her.

9

EXPECTING THE EARTH TO SHAKE

Another way some women push love out of their lives is to expect passion right away in a relationship. If they don't feel the earth shake, then they are not interested in a relationship. They are only interested in pursuing a relationship if they feel the spark of passion.

When a woman does not allow herself to feel her loss, she diminishes her ability to feel. She hungers to feel, but mistakenly believes that the right man will open her up. She does not realize that the feeling she is missing is suppressed within her. To the extent that she cannot feel the passion inside her, she will expect a man to ignite her romantic passions.

When a woman does not allow
herself to feel her loss,
she diminishes her ability to feel.

When a woman is not dealing with her suppressed feelings, going out with a nice guy who is interested in her is not very appealing. She needs to be in "relationship danger" to feel alive. There must be some dramatic tension for her to be in touch with her feelings. When there is danger, she is aroused. This danger could be physical, but it is emotional. She experiences the possibility of losing his love.

Some women need to be in
"relationship danger"
before they can feel fully alive.

Besides being a symptom of suppressed feelings, this excessive hunger for romance and passion is also encouraged in the movies and on TV. If a woman's favorite movie stars experience immediate passion, why can't she? It works in the movies, why not in her life?

Women who depend on a man to awaken their passion for living will continue to be disappointed. Maybe women in the movies get turned on right away but, in the real world, it takes time and loving communication. In real life, the women who find lasting love are not immediately aroused. The passion they eventually feel takes time to develop.

In real life it takes a woman time to
develop and experience passion.

This is not the same for a man. A man may feel the sexual passion right from the beginning. Men are wired differently. They first feel their sexual attraction, and gradually it develops into affection and then interest. Women are wired to experience interest first, and then sexual attraction. Women are first turned on in their minds.

When a woman experiences sexual attraction right away, it is clearly a sign that she is imagining in her mind that she already knows the man. When she eventually gets to know him, because he is not who she imagines him to be, she is disappointed. When a woman feels sexual attraction right away, it is clearly a warning signal.

When starting over, if a woman
meets a man who ignites her passion,
she should run the other way.

When a woman is attracted to finding passion, she lives in a world of disappointment. The only men that make her feel that passion are in some way dangerous. Like the mountain climber who needs danger to feel, the race car driver who needs speed, the alcoholic who needs a drink, this woman needs a man who is dangerous. She is automatically attracted to men who can hurt her in some way.

10

THE MOVIES VS. REAL LIFE

Another way some women push love out of their lives is to hold onto unrealistic expectations. This tendency is greatly encouraged by Hollywood. The big difference between the movies and real life is that in our homes we don't have professional writers who labor for months to help us find the right thing to say. Our partners are not professional actors who are capable of delivering perfect lines with perfect feeling and expression. We do not get the luxury of many "takes" and perfect lighting. In real life these writers and actors could never respond as they do in the movies.

Our partners are not professional actors
capable of delivering their perfect lines
with perfect delivery at the perfect time.

Not only are the scripts and actors unreal, the circumstances are overly exaggerated and choreographed to create maximum tension, which inevitably results in a passionate climax and release. In the movies, there is a build up of events that is not available in real life.

Having tasted the sweet ecstasy of passion in the movies, we say, "I want that." We return home and once again we are surrounded by a host of daily mundane chores. Suddenly the magic is gone. We look over at our partner and there is nothing but the usual. We long for the magic we felt watching the movie.

At home there are no battles,
no great heroes, no plagues,
and no miracle cures to evoke
passionate feelings of love.

Although movies are not real, what we feel in the movies is. It is possible to feel that passion. Otherwise, we would just laugh at it. We have that passion in our hearts. It is waiting to come out. Movies can help us to find what we are missing, but they don't teach us how to find passion in daily life. If we want to find that passion, we must learn to heal our hearts and regain our ability to feel and love fully. In addition, we need to take time to learn new relationship skills for creating romance.

11

ATTRACTING THE WRONG PARTNER

Many times a woman will get involved with a guy and all her friends say, "Watch out." Yet she ignores the obvious indicators that he is not there for her. Instead of turning away, she longs to win his love. She is setting herself up to be hurt. To the extent that she is dependent on her passion fix, she is not attracted to the man who is genuinely interested in her and respectful of her.

This tendency to be attracted to someone who is not capable of giving us what we want is the direct result of getting involved too soon. When we take time to heal our hearts, we are automatically attracted to partners who are closer to what we want and need. When we are still holding on to hurt, we tend to attract or be attracted to people who will hurt us again. This principle of attraction is true for both men and women.

When we are still holding on to hurt,
we will tend to attract or be attracted
to people who will hurt us again.

To the extent that we run away from our unresolved feelings, we will be attracted to situations
and people who will once again make us feel the
emotions we have not resolved. If we are still feeling hurt, then we may be attracted to someone
who could hurt us again. Although he is the
wrong person, he is the right person to link us
back to our unresolved feelings. If we use this
time to feel our feelings, we free ourselves from
this pattern of getting hurt again and again. When
we heal our hurt, we stop being attracted to the
wrong partners.

12

OVERROMANTICIZING

Another way some women push away love is by overromanticizing. They read romantic novels, watch romantic movies and soap operas, and then expect to experience this kind of romance in real life. They expect a man to be perfect.

Unless a woman's expectations
come back to earth, no real man
can ever satisfy her romantic
hopes and fantasies.

These women hold out for it all. They want a man who is a good listener, but who also opens up and shares his feelings. He is rich and committed to his work, but he has plenty of time for her and romance. He is a fine upstanding member of the community, and yet he is a rebel. He is daring and likes to take risks, but is grounded and secure. He has many interests and activities. He is his own person, unswayed by others, and yet he is always supportive of what she really wants. He is fiercely independent and autonomous, but he cannot live without her love. He is serious at the right times, but playfully spontaneous and entertaining at others. He is a tough, no-nonsense guy, but can also be compassionate and sensitive. He is everything good all rolled up in one person. When you read this list, I hope it becomes clear that this man doesn't exist.

Real romance does exist and is possible. It is not the result of being with a partner who has all these wonderful traits. Real romance occurs when we are able to nurture our partner's romantic needs. It does not require perfection at all. It does require that we learn and practice certain romantic skills. Most of all, it requires that we be in touch with our feelings.

Real and lasting romance does not require perfection.

When a woman is not in touch with her feelings, or her feelings from a past relationship are unresolved, then it will not be enough no matter what her partner does. Unresolved past feelings cause men and women to be dissatisfied with what they have. Instead of wanting what is possible, we demand of our partners what is unrealistic and end up feeling disappointed.

There is nothing wrong with wanting more in a relationship. We also need to be satisfied with what we are getting. To the extent we are not grateful for what we have, we are still suppressing unresolved feelings. When our hearts are open, we are able to love and appreciate what we have and keep wanting more. Wanting more only becomes a problem when what we are expecting and wanting is impossible and unrealistic.

13

WOMAN SEEKING SENSITIVE MAN

Another way women push love out of their lives is to require that a man be more like a woman. The mating call of the last thirty years for many women has been "Woman seeking sensitive man." Yet when they get one, he is never enough. Repeatedly, I have heard women claim how much they want a man who is in touch with his feelings, but then when they get him, they are dissatisfied. I have also met and worked with many angry men who say they are everything a woman supposedly wants, but then they are rejected for some "bad guy."

Once a woman gets a relationship with a "sensitive" man, she often complains that he is too sensitive. This does not mean that she doesn't love him, it is just a sore spot for her. She commonly feels as if she has to mother him or walk on eggshells around him. She gets turned off by his neediness.

It is not that something is wrong with a sensitive man. He just needs to learn how to manage his sensitivities in a way that allows her to get what she needs. On the other hand, she needs to learn how to reach her feelings without depending on him.

When a woman craves a man's
softness, it really is her own softness
that she is seeking to find.

When a woman is not in touch with her feelings, she will hunger for a man who is. She mistakenly believes that if he can open up, then she will be able to open up and connect. Unfortunately, this dependence is unhealthy. It really doesn't open her up. The more he opens up, the more responsible she feels for him. She feels there is little room to be herself in the relationship.

When a couple comes into counseling and the woman is complaining that her husband will not open up, the real problem is that she doesn't feel safe opening up. The solution to their problem is not helping the man to open up, but helping him to respect her feelings so that she can open up.

Certainly a man can benefit as well from opening up to his feelings. In healing a relationship, the first step is creating safety for the woman to feel and share her feelings. Without that, no matter what a man does it will never be enough for her. It is fine for a man to be sensitive, but he must also be strong. He must be capable of putting his feelings to the side when his partner needs him to listen and be there for her.

> When a woman does not feel
> safe to express her feelings,
> no matter what a man does,
> it will never be enough for her.

There are many women who complain to me that they feel their husbands are from Venus. The woman complains that her husband wants to do all the talking, and she doesn't have the time or the interest. He wants to work on their relationship, and she just wants to get away. He always wants to share feelings, and she wants to just solve the problem. This kind of role reversal creates its own set of problems to solve, but ultimately the solution is to find balance.

This man is still from Mars. He has just never seen a man successfully give a woman what she needs. By learning to listen first and not be argumentative, he begins to find his masculine power to make his partner feel more feminine. Though this is hard, in the beginning, as he builds his ability to "contain his feelings," he finds a new power and strength.

> By listening and containing his
> feelings, a man can build his
> masculine power to make
> his partner feel more feminine.

For a relationship to thrive, a woman needs support to feel feminine. Society is already conditioning women to be like men. When a woman gets home from work or after a long day raising a family without help, she needs some support to come back to feeling feminine. There is nothing more important to make a woman feel feminine than someone who is there for her, someone who cares, and someone who can listen and understand what she is going through.

Finding a sensitive man is not necessarily the remedy to this problem. What a woman needs today in a relationship is a man who will respect her feelings. Instead of being sensitive, he is sensitive *to* her feelings. The mating call of the next thirty years should ideally be "Woman seeking respectful man."

14

FOCUSING ON
THE NEGATIVE

Another common way women push love out of their lives is to focus on the negative. After a divorce or painful breakup, a woman may collect a variety of reasons and stories to justify not getting involved again. As long as no one else is really enjoying a loving relationship, then she is not really missing anything. Comforted by these "facts," she does not have to face her fears of getting hurt again.

If 50 percent of the people who get married each year get a divorce, she reasons, it can't be that great. Men also can fall prey to this pattern as well. Although this statistic is true, it does not account for the *millions* of couples who are still happily married and the thousands who get married each day who will live happily ever after. The argument against getting married really does not hold up when examined. If 50 percent of the people were rich, you wouldn't give up trying to make money.

> The odds for succeeding in
> marriage are actually very good—
> imagine if 50 percent of
> the people who go to Vegas
> won the jackpot.

As long as we are not willing to heal our negative feelings about past partners and relationships, we may have a negative attitude about the opposite sex. In this case, a woman may thrive on stories that validate her belief that you just can't trust a man and that you are better off without them. A man will tend to reason that women are just not worth the effort; no matter how much they get they are never satisfied. Neither of these attitudes is correct or conducive to finding a lifetime of love.

The more victim stories these women and men can hear and tell, the better they feel. If a woman is not directly healing her hurt, she begins to feed on this negativity. Ironically, by focusing on negativity, she really does find relief, but it is temporary. The negativity is really covering up the pain of her loneliness. To find real and lasting relief, she needs to heal the wounds she still carries in her heart.

Although joining a support group is almost always helpful, this person may just use the support group to stay stuck in negativity. She will generally benefit more from working privately with a therapist or practicing self-help exercises.

In addition, it is helpful to be exposed to positive stories about relationships, and to avoid talk shows that focus on how bad relationships can be. This kind of programming can just reinforce the bad habit of focusing on the negative.

15

WHO NEEDS A MAN?

When a woman waits too long to get involved again, she may become overly self-sufficient and unknowingly push love away. By not giving herself permission to need or depend on others, she closes the door to receiving love and support. Often she is afraid of appearing too needy, and so she compensates by not needing anyone. In her mind, she associates needing others with weakness. To open herself to love, a woman must be receptive to receiving support from others.

Men can also be vulnerable to this pattern, but not as much as women. A man will feel his need for a woman's love much more than a woman will feel her need for a man. When a woman can fulfill her physical needs without depending on a man, she may conclude that finding a man is more trouble than it is worth. She then affirms that she really doesn't need a man.

A man will feel his need for a woman's
love much more than a woman
will feel her need for a man.

A man will feel his need for sex and then be pulled back into the dating process. Feeling sexually attracted to a woman, he begins to open his heart and feel his need for love. Women, on the other hand, generally don't feel the pull of sexual attraction unless their hearts open first. The pull of sex doesn't automatically open their hearts. It is important for women to communicate their feelings in order to stay in touch with their receptivity.

Receptive feelings include trust, acceptance, and appreciation. When a woman denies her need for love, she loses touch with these receptive feelings and gradually becomes rigid and impervious to receiving support. She may not even realize it, but she is sending out a clear message: "I am strong. I don't need help." Besides being alone, she really loses touch with her ability to enjoy her life fully.

For a man to be attracted to a woman, he needs to feel that he can make a difference. When a woman disconnects from her receptive feelings by denying her needs, there is nothing to attract a man's desire to be there for her. Receptive feelings that attract a man are trust, acceptance, and appreciation. If a woman denies her needs, it sends out a message that she is not receptive.

Receptive feelings that attract a man
are trust, acceptance, and appreciation.

Besides pushing away a man's support, she will push away all support. When offered emotional support, she will immediately reject it, treating it as if it is not important or necessary. Ironically, quite often she is very happy to give support to others. Her problem is being able to receive it for herself. If she does not directly focus on feeling and healing her hurt after a loss, she will deny her needs to avoid the pain after the loss, making it increasingly difficult to receive love. Each time she begins to move into the receptive mode, she will start to feel her unresolved hurt feelings.

If needing love causes pain, she will just stop needing love to eliminate the pain. Instead of relying on the support of others or the hope of the support of others, she will take care of herself and all her needs. If she makes the shift to needing love again, she is forced to feel her unresolved hurt. Receiving love is then painful, because it causes her to feel her unresolved hurt once again.

If needing love causes pain, then a woman will just stop needing love to eliminate the pain.

To get out of this negative pattern, a woman needs to recognize that love does not mean pain. She needs to link her pain with her past and begin to heal it. She needs to find a therapist and to heal her loss. She needs to remember when in her childhood she really needed love and support and didn't get it. When an adult woman has problems with trust, it always stems from childhood issues. If she is too self-sufficient to see a therapist, then she can begin using self-help processes until she is open enough to receive the assistance of a therapist. By seeing a therapist, she is in fact affirming that she needs help. As she begins to trust and appreciate the benefits of therapy, she will begin to open her heart again.

There is certainly nothing wrong with being authentically self-sufficient, but there are some dangers. Women traditionally have depended on men for financial and physical support and protection. As women become more financially and physically self-sufficient, often they come to a crossroads. They no longer need a man for that support, so they wonder why they need a man at all.

Some women have come to a crossroads; they no longer need a man for financial support and so they wonder why they need a man at all.

Unless they are able to recognize why they need a man, they close the door to a man's support. If it really were true that they didn't need a man, then this would not be such a tragedy. The reality is that the more financially and physically self-sufficient a woman becomes, the more she begins to feel her need for emotional support from a man. The more successful she is, the more she hungers for companionship to receive emotional support and comfort.

Recognizing this is often a challenge. After

striving not to need a man for financial support, she realizes she needs a man for emotional support. Since this does not fit her image of herself, she hides this part of her in a closet. Exploring her feelings in a group can assist her in finding the part of her that needs support as well. Seeing other women opening up and receiving support encourages her so that she can do the same.

16

WOMEN WHO DO TOO MUCH

Many women push away love and support by taking on too much to do. They become so overwhelmed with the needs of others that they don't have time to feel or nurture their own needs. They don't feel comfortable asking for what they want, nor can they say no to the requests of others. They feel overly responsible for others, while at the same time they do not allow others to fill their own needs.

Although doing too much is frustrating, it does have emotional payoffs. First, by always being so busy, a woman can say no to others when necessary without feeling guilty. Second, if she is already doing everything she possibly can, then she is more entitled to ask for help. And third, as long as she is too busy to feel her own needs, she doesn't have to feel the pain of her loneliness and hurt.

A woman can avoid feeling her own pain by attending to the pain of others. It is certainly good to help others, but she must also take time to get the support she needs. By doing too much, she loses touch with herself and her own needs. Sharing her feelings assists her in coming back to herself and in feeling her own needs.

By doing too much, a woman loses
touch with herself and her own needs.

A woman who does too much will often resist the advice to share her feelings. She will say that she is too busy to talk about her feelings. There just isn't enough time for her. This problem will persist until she recognizes it as such. She has a problem. She needs to take time to get away and take care of her own needs, and then create time to explore her pain. Ideally, she can see a therapist to talk about the feelings that come up.

Although she is busy all the time, she is actually very lonely inside. She is giving, but she is not getting what she needs in return. Most important, she is not giving to herself. When a woman gives and gives to others but does not feel supported in her life, she will eventually become depressed.

Giving too much eventually
results in depression.

The major source of depression for women is feeling isolated. The more a woman pushes love away, the more isolated she feels. Eventually her ability to feel love, joy, appreciation, and trust diminishes. To avoid depression, a woman primarily needs to be heard. When her pain is heard, then her feelings of isolation go away and her loving and positive feelings have a chance to come back.

When a woman does too much, she knows the pain of others, but no one knows her pain. No one is there for her. Though she is particularly good at knowing what others need, she is not good at asking for what she needs. People just assume that she is strong and doesn't need help or that she is already getting it. Taking on too much, she becomes overwhelmed by attending to life's details. There is just too much to do and she feels she cannot do it all herself.

A woman who does too much
knows the pain of others, but
no one knows her pain.

Often, when a man is depressed, it is clear. He does not have energy to do anything. He is not motivated and he mopes around. Ultimately, the source of his depression is not feeling needed. A woman, on the other hand, feels depressed when she cannot get what she needs. As depression sets in, she often becomes acutely aware of the needs of others. Rather than becoming unmotivated, she feels more motivated, even obligated to be there for others.

She feels that she has to be there because no one else will. If she does create the time for a relationship, it is generally with a needy man who is also somewhat depressed and thus incapable of being there for her.

If he isn't already depressed, living with her could make him depressed. A man cannot thrive unless he feels that a woman is able to appreciate what he has to offer. A woman who does too much can zap a man's strength and power. In a similar manner, a depressed man who has nothing to offer a woman can drive her to doing too much.

When a woman does too much,
she can take a man's power.

Women who are stressed by life tend to do more and more. Men who are stressed by life will tend to have less energy to do more. A stressed man may have energy at work, but when he comes home he has nothing left. He is stuck to the couch and feels no energy or motivation.

A woman who is stressed by life will tend to come home and feel that a million things have to be done. She cannot relax her mind or forget her worries. The more she focuses on doing rather than feeling, she will feel a compulsion to do more, clean more, help more, and worry more. Eventually, her energy runs out and she is completely exhausted.

LEARNING TO DO LESS

This is clearly one area where men and women are very different. There are few men who have to learn how to do less. To do less, a woman needs training. A woman can learn to do less, but it doesn't happen right away. It takes these four stages:

In stage one, she needs to talk about her feelings, talk about her pain. She needs to complain. By opening up and sharing all that she is doing, she connects her feelings of exhaustion and her need to do less. Sharing enables her to feel the relief of not having to carry her burden completely alone. Communicating her feelings will eventually help her to relax and do less.

In stage two, she deliberately needs to do more things for herself, like getting a massage, seeing a therapist, going shopping for herself, or going on a little vacation. Besides giving herself a chance to relax and to enjoy her life, she also needs to experience that the world goes on without her. The sky doesn't fall when those things that "have" to get done don't get done.

Sometimes a woman will reject this advice, saying, "Yes, but if I take time for myself, then there is just more waiting for me when I get back." This is certainly true. Although it does build up, she should still take time off. Eventually she will see how she creates the urgency and then how she can change things.

In stage three, she needs to begin learning the art of asking for support. After preparing for this stage, she is now more capable of knowing what she needs so she can begin asking for support. Without this preparation she really doesn't even know what to ask for.

Taking time off for herself (stage two) actually forces her to begin asking for help. Without taking time off, she would not feel the need to ask for help. In her mind, it is more difficult to ask or depend on others than it is to do it herself. The art of learning to ask for support is covered in great detail in Chapter Twelve of *Men Are from Mars, Women Are from Venus*.

In stage four, she can begin to say no gracefully to the needs and requests of others. One of a woman's biggest obstacles to doing less is that she doesn't know how to say no lovingly. Certainly she can say no, but she doesn't know how to say it gracefully and comfortably. By learning to ask for support, she will eventually become more comfortable saying no to others. By deliberately practicing the art of saying no, it will become much easier. All she is has to say is, "I am so sorry, I can't." If she still doesn't feel comfortable saying no and continues to do too much, she must look deeper into her feelings to create a change.

A woman's resistance to saying no often comes from unresolved feelings toward someone who said no to her needs. Since she knows the pain of her needs being rejected, she cannot bear rejecting another. If she has been abandoned, she doesn't want to abandon someone else. To change her pattern she will need to heal the unresolved hurt from her past.

To the extent that her past feelings are unresolved she will have difficulty both saying no and asking for more. She will avoid asking for more because she doesn't want to feel the hurt of being denied. She will have a difficult time saying no because she doesn't want to hurt another.

> Since her past pain is still unresolved,
> she will be overly sensitive to
> the needs of others.

Rather than feel her pain linked to needing help and being denied, she would rather do everything herself. As long as her pain remains unhealed, her fear of being hurt or causing hurt will keep her from comfortably asking for support and saying no to doing more. She will feel inappropriately responsible for the needs of others to such an extent that there is no time to relax.

To heal her past, she needs to remember times when her needs were unrecognized, invalidated, or unfulfilled. By taking time to explore her feelings, eventually she will be able to feel appropriate anger and blame, and then to practice forgiveness. She must be careful, though, not to practice forgiving and understanding right away.

A forgiving and understanding attitude can sometimes be an easy way to avoid the painful truth that we are hurt and in pain. It is not uncommon to suppress our feelings by saying things like, "It's okay. It's all right, I understand." On the other hand, these are powerfully healing statements.

> A forgiving and understanding
> attitude can sometimes be an easy
> way to avoid the painful truth that
> we are hurt and in pain.

When a woman is too selfless, it means that she was hurt by someone in her past, by someone who was too selfish, needy, demanding, or simply irresponsible. To develop a healthy sense of responsibility, she needs to feel her anger and forgive. She needs to feel her sorrow that she couldn't get what she wanted, but also to recognize that she was not responsible.

Until she has healed this pattern, she could easily remain single and without support. In her mind, if there is no time for her, then there is no time for a man in her life.

If a woman has this tendency at the end of a relationship, then usually it was there since her childhood. This may skew her desire to experience intimacy again. If in her past relationship she didn't have time for herself, then she doesn't have a picture of how loving and nurturing a relationship can be. Unless she gets a more positive picture of what is possible, she may decide never to get involved again.

17

TAKING CARE
OF OTHERS

A common way women push away opportunities to find love is to lose themselves in serving others who are in greater need. Though serving others is a good thing, it can also be a way to avoid feeling their own needs. It is hard to feel sorry for yourself when others have problems greater than your own.

I am not suggesting that a woman should feel sorry for herself, but she does need to take time to mourn her loss. When a woman doesn't feel safe to share her feelings, then she begins to feel sorry for herself. To avoid sinking into the depths of self-pity, she helps others. It is a good thing to help others, but not if she is avoiding her own healing process.

To avoid sinking into the
depths of self-pity, a woman will
seek to help others.

It is actually very helpful for a wounded man to help others who are in need. It will assist him in feeling his own pain and doing something about it. The more a man feels he is needed, the more he is able to overcome and heal his personal pain. By experiencing the pain of others, a man actually becomes more in touch with his own feelings and needs. As a result, he is empowered to do something to get his needs met.

The opposite holds true for women. Women can easily lose themselves through serving the needs of others. A woman in the process of healing her heart needs to be especially careful not to take on new responsibilities. She must take time to feel her needs and get her needs met. Otherwise, she will never heal her hurt and will be dependent on taking care of others to escape her pain.

THE DESIRE TO HAVE CHILDREN

When a woman feels powerless to get the love she needs, she may feel a premature desire to have children. Just like the women who depend too much on their children for love, she will seek to have children. It is so easy to get love from a child. Rather than face the responsibility of creating an adult relationship, she seeks the love of children. The thought of having children reassures her that she can and will be loved. This same need can be satisfied in a healthier manner by taking care of a pet. She can nurture a pet without feeling the pressure of taking care of a child.

This does not imply that a woman's desire for children is always for this reason. If she is young, single, and wanting children, it could be that she is avoiding intimacy by seeking the love of children without having to face the challenges of an intimate relationship. To have children before her heart is healed will not only prevent her from getting the love she needs, but it is also not fair to the children.

Rather than looking to children for love, she needs to learn how to get love from friends, family, and then a partner. When she is full from her adult relationships, then she is ready to overflow with unconditional love. Then she is most prepared for having children of her own.

18

A WOMAN'S FEAR OF INTIMACY

To the extent that she is afraid of intimacy, a woman will be attracted to a man who is not fully available to her. Deep inside, she wants love, but she is also afraid of getting hurt again.

When a man is interested and available to her, her fears keep her from feeling attracted. She does not consciously think, "Okay, I don't want to get involved, so let me find some reasons why I don't want to be with this person." It just happens automatically. Suddenly, as she gets closer, her fears cause her to become overly critical and judgmental.

If she is with a man who is not available, then it is suddenly safe to love. All her pent-up feelings of love come up. Ironically, if the man who was not available becomes free, then her feelings of attraction may suddenly disappear. As soon as a man is available, her fears come up and she rejects him.

This fear of intimacy can be healed gradually.

On one level a woman needs to date, but to go slow. By making sure she is not looking for a marriage partner or a sexual partner, she can begin to heal her fears of intimacy.

At another level, she needs to explore the unresolved feelings left from her last relationship. While exploring and resolving her feelings, it is most powerful and helpful for her to link her feelings to earlier and earlier experiences. By going back, she is able to heal the deeper levels of her fear, which generally stem from occasions when our parents hurt, betray, or disappoint us in some way. By processing her fear of abandonment and rejection, she will eventually be attracted to men who are available.

19

MY CHILDREN NEED ME

A woman pushes love away by prioritizing the needs of her children over her own needs. After a divorce or a death, a woman feels the need to be both parents. She knows that a child needs two parents, so she compensates and tries to give more. Though this is a noble gesture, it prevents her from reaching out and getting the love she needs from another adult.

If she is in pain from her loss, this natural tendency to sacrifice herself for her children is reinforced even more. As we have already explored, a woman already tends to escape her pain by caring for the needs of others. If she does not take time to heal her pain, then nurturing her children can be the perfect escape from her own pain.

By focusing on the needs of her children, she is able to avoid facing her fears of looking for love once again. By busying herself in the process of parenting, she can easily suppress her own needs for intimacy and love. Although she may be fulfilled parenting her children, she will be pushing love out of her life. This is not healthy for herself or for her children.

By busying herself in the process of parenting, a woman can easily suppress her own needs for intimacy and love.

Although it seems as if she is giving more to her children, they will end up feeling the burden and responsibility of making her happy.

All children want to make their mothers happy, but a grown woman has other needs that a child cannot meet. She has adult needs for intimacy, sharing, understanding, cooperation, companionship, affection, reassurance, encouragement, and romance. When a woman does not take responsibility to fulfill these adult needs, her children automatically will feel an added burden. They will begin to feel the pressure she is avoiding. They will take on an inappropriate sense of responsibility for fulfilling her adult needs.

What children need most is for their mother to be fulfilled.

In their attempt to make her happy, they will fail. Children cannot fulfill an adult's needs. No matter how much she loves them, if she is not taking responsibility to fulfill herself, then her children will suffer, experiencing a variety of problems later in life.

Most commonly, when children take too much responsibility for a parent's happiness, they become people pleasers and accommodaters. As children, they had to give up a part of themselves to please their mother. This pattern continues into adulthood. They continue to sacrifice too much, and then later resent that they didn't get what they needed. They have a hard time separating their own needs from the needs of others, which makes them feel overly responsible for others. As a result, they end up giving too much.

Children of unfulfilled mothers
often become people pleasers,
accommodaters, and people
who give too much.

A child who feels the weight of responsibility too early may feel this pressure and fold. He will simply swing the other way. Instead of trying to please his mother, he stops caring. This is very hard on a child, because once he disconnects from the basic urge to please his parents, he loses direction in his life. Not knowing what he wants, he is easily influenced by others. Such children conform to their crowd and want what others want or what they see on TV. They do not know what they want.

When a little boy is unable to make his mother happy, he will be more frustrated when his female partner is unhappy about something as an adult. Instead of reacting with compassion, he reacts defensively and becomes overly frustrated or angry. He cannot tolerate the thought that here is another woman he cannot please.

A little girl may either become like her mother or react by denying her inner needs. She does not want to burden someone else the way her mother burdened her. Unfortunately, her denial of her needs will frustrate her male partner. He will not feel as if he can connect with her. The more he tries, the more she pulls away. She will have a difficult time asking for what she wants because she doesn't want to be a burden on others. Holding herself to these standards, she can be very hard on herself and others.

THE HEALTHY RELATIONSHIP BETWEEN PARENT AND CHILD

The healthy relationship between parent and child is unconditional love. The parents give and the children receive. When love is unconditional, children feel that they don't have to give back. They are not responsible for their parents. As a result, a child learns to give not because he should, but because he wants to. As long as children do not feel responsible for parents, they can want to please their parents in a healthy way.

When children are successful in pleasing their parents while growing up, they do not grow up feeling like people pleasers. They have a strong sense of who they are, along with a healthy desire to be of service to others.

It is okay if the parent is not happy all the time or goes unfulfilled for some time. As long as the parent does not look to the children, but takes responsibility for his own adult needs, the child is free from feeling the burden of responsibility.

This important insight helps any single parent adjust her priorities in a healthy manner. Instead of prioritizing the needs of her children, she needs to prioritize her own needs first and then her children's needs. This is not license to ignore a child's need, but it does give a single parent the necessary wisdom and permission to take care of her own needs first.

DATING AND SINGLE PARENTS

When a single parent wants to go out on a date, often he or she will feel guilty. She will feel that she should spend more time with her children. She can sense that her children want more and she feels guilty leaving. What single parents don't know is that even if they were still married their children would want more.

It is a child's job to want more and a parent's job to set reasonable limits. *Reasonable limits* means that parents must make sure that they are not sacrificing their needs for their children.

If a parent is not setting reasonable limits, then a child's wants and needs will become unreasonable.

The child will push until she finds the limit. Giving too much or sacrificing your own needs may feel like love, but it really doesn't support your child. Certainly we do make loving sacrifices for our children at times, but we must then balance things out and take time for ourselves. If a parent denies her own needs, a child never gets a clear example of how to set limits in his own life.

One of the greatest challenges of single parenting is continuing to nurture your own adult needs. With this insight into what children really need, single parents can make the right decisions for themselves and for their children.

20

BUT MY CHILDREN
ARE JEALOUS

Single parents commonly push love away by being overly concerned that their children will be jealous or upset with them for getting involved again. Yes, their children will be jealous, but that is not a good reason to avoid love. It is actually another reason a parent *should* get involved in a relationship.

When a parent gets involved again, it helps a child to face his own loss as well. It also frees the child from feeling responsible for the parent. Rather than protecting her children from being jealous, a single parent needs to focus on helping her children deal with and overcome their jealousy when it comes up.

Rather than protecting their children
from being jealous, a single parent
needs to focus on helping her children
deal with and overcome their jealousy.

When single parents become seriously involved, engaged, or remarried, often they protect their children from feeling jealous by downplaying their affection for their new partner while in front of the children. Though this might seem like a good idea, it is not. Instead, they should make a special and deliberate point to talk up their new partner.

Instead of playing down our love and
affection, we should deliberately
express it in front of our children.

The children need to have reason to like this intruder. They have not gone out and picked him. Children are usually very happy to have the single parent all to themselves. If they hear, see, and experience in a variety of ways that the new person makes Mommy or Daddy very happy, then they will begin to welcome the new partner.

Every child eventually likes someone
who makes their parent happy.

When a child resents the involvement of a step-parent, it is appropriate to create special times to be with the child without the stepparent. Just as the new couple has private time together, the children should feel that they will also get to have some special and private time with the parent.

Parents, whether divorced or not, often make the child the center of their lives. To counter this tendency, we must take special efforts to prioritize adult needs.

FITS AND TANTRUMS

In reaction to a new partner, a child may throw fits and tantrums of jealousy. The wise parent is able to listen patiently and compassionately, because he or she understands their pain. The wise parent is able to recognize that the expression of these feelings is a necessary adjustment and that it will pass. Some children by nature are more dramatic than others and will be more outwardly expressive of their inner pain.

When a child doesn't like the new person, a parent needs to remember that it really isn't personal. The child is still angry that Mom and Dad are divorced, and that anger comes out on the new person. Until a child's hurt, anger, and fear are healed, he may not like anyone you pick. Instead of trying to convince a child that the new partner is likable, a parent should focus more on helping the child feel and express her loss.

Instead of trying to convince a child
that the new partner is likable, a parent
should focus more on helping the child
feel and express his/her loss.

If a parent has difficulty validating a child's pain, she needs to remember that it is not the child's decision. The child did not go out and pick this person. She does not necessarily love him or like him. When an outsider comes into the family, he is an intrusion. He is a threat, someone who has come between the child and her parent.

In my workshops for young children, I have witnessed over and over that more than anything, children want Mommy and Daddy to love each other. When drawing pictures of what makes them happy, they almost always draw a picture of Mommy and Daddy loving each other. One big happy family makes them happiest and most secure.

When someone else comes into the picture, they are forced to recognize that Mommy and Daddy are not getting back together. They are forced to face their feelings of loss. Until you bring someone home, your children are often hoping that Mommy and Daddy will get back together.

EXPECT JEALOUSY

When we are ready to get involved again, we should expect that our children will be upset and be pleasantly surprised if they are not. Even though the parent is ready, the child may still have unresolved feelings. We should simply expect jealousy. To the extent that a child has not dealt with his feelings of loss, he will be jealous of a new partner in some way.

By helping our children to deal with jealous feelings, we will be helping them face and deal with their other feelings of loss. Unresolved hurt, anger, and fear will automatically come up. Just as *we* need to heal the hurt of our loss, they too must face their feelings. If we have faced ours, it helps them enormously.

One child will often express the feelings for all the children. How you deal with one will greatly affect the others. We must be careful not to make comments to one child minimizing another child's feelings. The nonjealous child may even make his own comments to put down another child's feelings. It is important that we stand up for and validate everyone's feelings.

One child will often express the
feelings for all the children.

If we cannot deal patiently with our children's feelings, it is often a sign that we still have unresolved feelings. We resist their feelings because we are still resisting certain feelings within ourselves. To the extent that we suppress our feelings about a breakup, our children will feel and act out those feelings. Certainly they have their own issues, but what we suppress will be added onto their feelings.

Our children will express or act out
what we are still suppressing.

This does not mean that we should share our painful feelings with our children. This is clearly not appropriate. Children should never feel that they are a sounding board for our pain. If we use them it this manner, they will feel even more responsible for our needs. Instead of getting to be children and to grow up naturally, our neediness can force them to be adults right away.

What we feel does not hurt our children as long as we take responsibility to deal with it. It does not hurt our children if we are devastated by our loss, as long as they are not made to feel responsible for us in any way. It is fine for them to see us sad or upset, but only to a degree. We must remember that they are very sensitive and will begin to feel responsible for us.

Ultimately what frees them from feeling responsible for us is the degree to which we are nurturing ourselves. When we are taking responsibility to help ourselves and get support from family, friends, groups, or therapy, our children are released from carrying our weight.

21

ACTING OUT FEELINGS RATHER THAN COMMUNICATING

After a loss, women may push love out of their lives by acting out their feelings. Instead of taking time to explore and communicate their feelings, women often express them through behavior. This acting out is not a conscious decision, but often a compulsion.

To the degree that she doesn't feel safe
to express her feelings, a woman will
begin acting them out.

If in her past relationship she has felt ignored and neglected, she will dress in a manner that clearly says, "Look at me, I am unattractive. No one would ever love me." Her unresolved feelings lead her to stop caring for herself or her appearance.

If a way she cared for herself in the past was to regulate her diet and weight, she will have great difficulty continuing her program. To the extent that she feels no one cares about her, she has a difficult time being motivated to care about herself.

This apathy often occurs when a woman has the tendency to blame herself too much. She does not give herself permission to feel angry about her loss, and as a consequence she blames herself. When there is no one else to blame, we blame ourselves. Unless she is able to change this tendency, her suppressed anger fuels her apathy.

When a woman does not give
herself permission to feel angry,
she blames herself.

She is trapped feeling sorry for herself with no one to blame. As she continues to neglect herself, this false belief that it is all her fault gets reinforced. Certainly no one else is to blame if she overeats or mistreats herself. Her acting out reinforces her feelings of unworthiness and the quality of her life spirals downward.

She can break free from this pattern by allowing herself to be angry about her loss. By linking her present feelings with feelings in her past, she can more effectively get in touch with her suppressed feelings.

GOING OUT OF CONTROL

Often when a woman stops caring for herself, she is acting out her feelings of powerlessness. She will generally feel powerless to reach out to get the love and support she needs. If she cannot share her feelings, she then acts out in manner that says to all, "I am out of control. I am powerless. I need help."

When we cannot grieve our sorrow,
then automatically we act out in ways
that express our powerlessness.

Instead of losing control in her adult life to feel and heal her feelings of powerlessness, she can instead remember as a child when she really was powerless to get the love and support she needed. By taking time to remember and explore incidents in which she really was powerless, she can release the tendency to lose control in her adult life.

LETTING GO OF RESENTMENT

Another reason a woman stops caring for herself is that she is acting out her unresolved feelings of resentment. After years of caring for another and not getting back what she needed, she is empty. She has nothing left to give. She has done everything she could to give and receive love and it hasn't worked. She now feels resentful and exhausted.

She refuses to keep trying to get love. She stops doing anything that would be associated with attracting love into her life. In a spirit of defiance, she will stop taking care of herself so that she will be clearly unattractive and unworthy of someone's love and affection. She will deliberately reject the attempts of others to help her. Her defiance is her statement that she clearly does not trust love, nor will she ever be fooled by it again. She has decided that she does not need love and will do nothing to get it. This is her way of expressing how she feels.

A woman's defiance is her statement
that she clearly does not trust love, nor
will she ever be fooled by it again.

Until she is able to feel and release the hurt feelings under her resentment, her problems will just get worse. To reach out and get support would mean that she wants to find love again. Even to consider that brings up her painful feelings of hurt, rejection, betrayal, and deprivation. As long as she does not consider getting involved again or depending on love, she does not have to face those feelings.

REVENGE HELPS NOBODY

When a woman feels resentful and powerless, she may act these feelings out through revenge if she is unable to communicate them. Revenge helps no one. To the extent that she seeks revenge she will make unfortunate decisions and choices that will affect the rest of her life. By seeking revenge, she mistakenly believes she will find satisfaction.

When a man seeks revenge, he wants someone to feel the pain he feels. He has been hurt and he wants someone to pay. He feels, "I want you to feel the hurt you caused me." Certainly a woman may feel this way, but more commonly, instead of wanting her ex-partner to hurt as she hurts, she will want him to feel really bad about what he has done. Her revenge is different. Even when she clearly wants him to hurt, the underlying need is for him to feel responsible for hurting her.

A woman seeks revenge by
wanting her ex-partner to
feel really bad for hurting her.

When a man seeks revenge by saying and doing mean things, he deliberately wants to hurt his ex-partner in some way. When a woman says or does mean things, it is to tell the world that he is bad. She feels, "I want everyone to know what he did." Basically she wants him and everyone else to share her feelings that he is really bad.

Her true need is to be heard. She needs others to hear and validate her pain. She needs to heal the hurt she feels inside. Her need to tell the world about him is her indirect attempt to tell the world how she feels. She reasons, "If you know what he did, then you will know what I feel."

This indirect approach provides temporary relief, but it does not heal. To heal her hurt she must feel it, put it into words, share it, and then be heard.

**Underlying revenge is the need
to share our pain.**

Seeking revenge only makes matters worse for ourselves. When a man seeks to hurt someone, besides ending up in jail, he only hurts himself because he is disconnecting from his most noble spirit. A man is most fulfilled when he seeks to be of service and to protect. As long as his motive is to hurt another, he is disconnected from his higher purpose.

When a woman seeks to make a man feel guilty or bad for what he has done, she disconnects from her ability to appreciate the opportunities she does have to move on and be happy. When she focuses on making him feel guilty, she must affirm once again how he has devastated her life. To get the sympathy for which she is looking, she must continue to be a victim.

**To make another feel bad, we must
continue to be victims.**

If her husband left her for another woman, she must remain alone, destitute, and unhappy to get sympathy. If she suddenly met and married Prince Charming, she would have little to complain about. If she was to move on and be happy, then that would mean it was a good thing that the relationship ended. To justify the sympathy she seeks, she may spend the rest of her life refusing to be happy.

If a woman suddenly met and married Prince Charming, she would have little to complain about.

Refusing to be happy in order to get revenge, a woman sabotages her own ability to find love. As long as she holds on to her hurt to make her ex-partner feel bad, then she cannot let go of her resentment with forgiveness. Stuck in her hurt feelings, she is unable to trust that she will ever find love again. Although she may feel she is punishing her ex-partner, she is really punishing herself.

22

LEARNING TO BE HAPPY ALONE

A woman is trained from childhood to hide her unpleasant feelings. She is taught to be desirable and not to desire. This training conflicts with her feelings of loss. Her conditioning says, if you want love, then be happy, but her authentic need is to share her hurt feelings. After a loss, she hides the part of her that needs love the most. She ends up suppressing her feelings to be lovable. Unfortunately, no matter how much love she gets, this way she will never feel loved.

To get love, she denies her negative feelings and tries to be happy. She does not know that her honest feelings of loss do not in any way make her unlovable. To be lovable, she attempts to be happy on her own. Ironically, to get love, she ends up being alone. Trying to be happy and positive about her loss, she suppresses and denies her hurt feelings, obstructs the healing process, and eventually pushes away opportunities to find love.

A part of her wants to be positive, but another part of her just wants to cry in someone's arms. This goes against everything she has been taught.

When a woman needs love the most, she may be unable to reveal the feelings that need to be heard for her to be loved.

She has learned that if she wants to be loved she needs to be loving, accepting, appreciative, friendly, warm, responsible, giving, accommodating, and happy. If she doesn't have something nice to say, then she shouldn't say anything at all. This kind of conditioning and programming makes it very difficult for her to be honest about her feelings. After years of learning to put on emotional makeup to be more desirable, she becomes so good at covering up that sometimes she fools herself as well.

After years of putting on emotional makeup, a woman can fool herself as well.

She tells others that she is fine, and she believes it herself. Instead of taking time to feel her sadness for what she is missing, she tells herself that everything is okay. To avoid feeling the pain of her loss, she begins to look at the positive. She idealizes her life. She focuses on how much easier and happier she is without a partner.

BEING HAPPY WITHOUT A MAN

When a woman practices being happy without a man, she must be careful that she is also honestly dealing with her hurt. It is very easy for a woman to disconnect from her need for a man. If she works at being content without a man *and* also takes time to deal with her unhappy feelings of loss, then she will be opening the door to find intimacy again.

As we discussed before, the best time to get involved is when we are content without a partner. We are most likely to find a partner when we are not desperately looking for one or depending on one to be happy. Women have to be particularly careful that their contentment is real and not a cover-up to avoid facing their feelings of anger, sadness, fear, or sorrow.

The best time to get involved
again is when we are content
without a partner.

When a woman becomes comfortable in the state of denying her feelings, she runs the risk of remaining alone the rest of her life. By continuing to suppress her wounded feelings, eventually a portion of her feminine self, which needs love, becomes repressed. Her masculine side comes forward to take care of her needs, assuming the role of a man in her life.

When a woman repeatedly suppresses her hurt feelings, they finally go away. She finds permanent relief, but not healing. While she may experience freedom from pain, it comes at a price. While she is happy, she cannot fully feel it.

To the extent that we repress our pain,
our ability to feel anything is restricted.

She becomes comfortable in her life and doesn't feel the need for a partner. She feels it might be nice to have someone to see movies with or occasionally go on a vacation with, but that's about it. The part of her that genuinely needs love the most is buried. Until her wounds are healed, a part of her will continue to live without love and she will not even know that she is missing something.

When and if she does decide to get involved again, it may be difficult to attract a man. Until she is able to face the part of herself that needs love, it is difficult for a man to be that attracted to her.

When a woman is willing to unlock
the doorway to her heart,
then men will come knocking.

A woman needs to allow herself to be unhappy. If this is hard, she can set aside a little time each day to be unhappy. If she doesn't want anyone to know, she can start out sharing these negative feelings by writing in a journal. Eventually, as she becomes more comfortable looking at her wounded feelings, it is advisable for her to join a support group or find a therapist with whom she can share this part of herself.

23

ALL OR NOTHING

Some women push away love by demanding everything right away. They are unwilling to take the necessary time to date and slowly get to know someone. This type of woman wants everything out on the table right away. She doesn't want to play any games. No pretending. She says it like it is, and that's that. If a man can't handle her directness, then that's too bad. She is not interested. He had better accept her the way she is, or she's out of there.

If a man can't handle her the way she is, then she would rather be alone. This attitude may make her feel strong, but it is not very loving to herself. She will never find love being so opinionated, rigid, and inflexible. Her no-nonsense approach seems admirable and desirable, but it doesn't work.

Although her power seems authentic, it is not. Real power is the ability to get what we need. Although she wants to be strong and loving, she does not know what that means. She needs love just like everyone else, but her fear keeps her from giving a relationship a chance. To find true and lasting love, she needs to recognize that her all-or-nothing attitude is very limiting to herself and others.

A woman's tough exterior often hides a
very sensitive, hurt woman.

Her unwillingness to accommodate a man is a sign that in the past she has tried everything and it hasn't worked. Her apparent lack of accountability is really based upon years of trying to be accountable. She has given in completely in the past, so now she will not budge an inch. She feels she has wasted years trying to please others, giving of herself but not getting back. She wisely seeks to find balance, but swings too far in the other direction.

She wants to share everything right away because she has little ability to delay gratification. She must have it all now or she is not interested. This emotional neediness is similar to the behavior of a child. A child wants it all, and she wants it now. To nurture and heal this childlike part of her, this woman needs to learn how to delay gratification without giving up.

This ability to delay gratification will develop when the woman takes time to heal her wounds. She is longing to put her feelings on the table because her pain is crying to be heard. Starting a relationship is not the appropriate context to do this healing. She must be careful not to confuse being in an intimate relationship with therapy.

Before she is ready for a relationship, she needs to take time in therapy or a support group to look at her past issues with men and heal her hurt.

Starting a relationship is not the appropriate context to heal our past relationships.

Wanting to share everything right away is like a man wanting to have sex right away. Imagine how foolish and immature it would sound if a man said, "I want to have sex right away. If you can't handle that, then I'm out of here. I want what I want, and if I can't have it on my terms, forget it." A woman seeking to be emotionally intimate right away is as impulsive and immature as a man demanding sex. Recognizing her neediness in this light will help her not to justify it.

Her impulsiveness also reveals a lack of understanding of how love grows. Her insight into the process of dating is very limited. She would benefit greatly by learning about the five stages of dating described in *Mars and Venus on a Date*. With a clear understanding of how love grows, she will be able to realize her potential to find true and lasting love.

HOW LOVE GROWS

A relationship unfolds in degrees. When you plant a seed it takes time to grow. You don't demand results right away. People need time to get to know each other. If we rush this process, we may derail a perfectly good relationship.

When a woman rushes intimacy, often the man feels a sudden need to get away. His retreat fuels her neediness and she pushes him away. By first dating around with several men and not becoming exclusive or intimate right away, a woman can begin to curb this tendency to merge immediately. Although merging feels natural and it is what she wants, she must restrain herself if she is to nurture a relationship. Love cannot grow when we smother it with too much intimacy too soon.

By dating around with several men,
a woman can begin to curb her
tendency to merge right away.

To move into an intimate relationship, a woman needs to make sure that her life stays intact. A needy woman will tend to make a man the center of her life and then require him to satisfy all her needs. Although he may feel flattered, he will eventually run for the hills. It is unrealistic to expect any man to fulfill all of a woman's needs. With patience and the wisdom of restraint, a woman can eventually overcome her emotional neediness.

MAKING A MAN THE CENTER OF HER LIFE

To overcome her emotional neediness, a woman must make sure that she doesn't make a man the center of her life. She can learn to contain her neediness by being careful to go slow and make sure that she continues to feel supported by her relationships with friends and family. It is a mistake to drop everything for an intimate relationship with a man.

The love and support of her friends and family is just as important as the love of a man. In some ways it is actually much more important. The support she receives from family and friends provides the basis for having a relationship with a man. With this foundation of support, she doesn't require too much from a man, nor does she tend to give too much.

> The love and support of her friends
> is like having a good home-cooked
> dinner, and a man's love is a
> delicious dessert.

Without common sense grounded in the wisdom of how love grows, it is easy for a woman to follow her instincts and then be disappointed. When her friends tell her to hold back to get a man's love and attention, she resists. She doesn't want to play any games. She does not realize that holding back in this situation is not manipulation, it is wisdom.

Without insight into the various stages of dating, she just shoots from her hip. Holding back is not what she feels like doing, so she plunges forward. In the name of being authentic, she follows her every impulse without restraint. Imagine someone who drinks too much or overspends using this approach. As long as he follows his impulses, his life will continue to spiral downward and his bank accounts will stay empty.

To succeed in starting over, we must be careful that we do not justify our own neurosis in the name of being authentic. Being respectful of the dating process does not mean that we are playing games. Ultimately, being authentic is what makes a relationship work, but we must reveal all of who we are in degrees.

PLAYING GAMES

Although playing games doesn't work, wisdom does. When a woman adamantly resists "playing games," it is generally because either she has played them in the past and they didn't work or someone played games with her and she was hurt. If she is still hurt, she is reacting to her past and not giving a new relationship a chance.

When a woman adamantly resists
"playing games," she may be throwing
out the baby with the bathwater.

The games people play often contain nuggets of truth. Most of the games women play to seduce a man are actually based on practical wisdom. Wisdom facilitates the growth of love, while games of seduction justify deception. Often when a woman uses deception to get a man, when she finally gets him, she loses him. When he discovers who she really is, he may discover that he does not really love her.

These are some examples of manipulative games that don't work and good advice that does. Although they are similar, they are worlds apart.

Manipulative Games	Good Advice
Don't return his calls and he will want you more.	Don't make a man the center of your life. Return his calls but don't drop everything for him.
Be sexy, dress sexy, do everything he wants in bed.	Dress in a way that makes you feel good, and don't have sex until you are ready.
Hide your real feelings, remain cool and aloof. Don't be eager in any way.	Hold back from sharing all your feelings right away. Be careful not to rush things. Let the flower unfold one petal at time.
Don't call a man or seem too interested.	It is fine to call a man, but don't expect him to have a lot to say, and if he does be pleasantly surprised. And don't ask a lot of questions. Instead, share your thoughts and feelings.

Date around to make him jealous.	By dating around, but not sleeping around, it will free you from being too needy for his attention.
Don't be too available; say you are too busy sometimes.	Make sure that you are not waiting for his call. Keep busy in your life so you are not too needy.
Dress, speak, smile, flirt in a manner to seduce a man.	Be careful to not pursue a man more than he is pursuing you. It is his job to seduce you; it is your job to attract his interest. A woman can easily seduce a man, but rarely will he commit.

MEN ARE FROM MARS, WOMEN ARE FROM VENUS

Although it sounds good to be direct and put it all out on the table, this kind of attitude reveals an insensitivity to others and their needs. This kind of woman often has little tolerance for differences. She thinks her way is right and a man should think, feel, and react the way she does. This woman needs to read *Men Are from Mars, Women Are from Venus*. She needs to realize and recognize that men are different. Men and women are different and we are supposed to be that way.

In the next section, we will explore many of the

unique challenges that men experience when starting over. Although the examples are addressed to men, there is still some overlap. Many women may find patterns or parts of patterns they also experience. By taking time to understand the male perspective, a woman will get a glimpse of what men are going through when they start over. This will help her to make sense of her experiences and assist her in making wise decisions to facilitate the growth of love in her life.

PART THREE

Starting Over on Mars

Starting over on Mars has its own unique challenges. It can be like walking through a field of land mines. Some are lucky and get through, but others get blown to bits. Hearing the mistakes of others will enable you to make the right choices for yourself. With greater insight, you will have the confidence and the wisdom to march forward without making the same mistakes others have made before you.

In each of the following twenty-three examples, you may find a little piece of yourself. By relating to the challenges of others, although they may be different in some way, you will gain a greater insight into what is required to navigate your own path as you start over. By getting the support you need and making the right decisions, you will be able to bring forward the best of who you are and to experience the fullness of love and power expressed in a meaningful relationship.

1

MAN ON THE REBOUND

One of biggest differences between men and women starting over is that men tend to get involved too soon, while women take too long. A man on the rebound moves from one relationship to another. He does not realize that by doing this he misses the opportunity to heal his heart. Getting involved after a loss may soothe his pain, but it does little to heal it.

Without an understanding of how to grieve a loss, a man will simply feel his pain and then go out and solve the problem. Men are problem solvers. They don't feel comfortable sitting around "feeling their feelings." If a man feels the pain of not having money, then he goes out and makes some. If he feels the pain of losing a woman's love, he goes out and finds a woman to love him.

When a man gets involved right
away, he misses the opportunity
to heal his heart.

A man on the rebound doesn't realize that another woman's love will not heal his heart. Her love will soothe his soul and bring up his painful feelings to be healed. He must take responsibility to feel his pain, not run away from it. He must feel the four healing emotions until his pain goes away. This doesn't mean that he bears it all alone either. This is a time for him to reach out to friends and family for support.

The best time for a man to get deeply involved again is when he doesn't have to. As long as he feels he "has" to be in a relationship to escape his pain, he is not ready to make a commitment. When a man on the rebound makes a commitment, it is hard for him to keep it. Eventually, he will either wonder why he can't make up his mind, or he will clearly decide that his partner is the wrong one for him. Most rebound relationships do not last.

When a man gets involved
on the rebound, his commitment
is rarely lasting.

A hungry man will eat almost anything. After his immediate hunger is satisfied, he can then afford to be more picky about what he wants. A man on the rebound is like a man starving for food. He can fall in love with almost anyone who offers him a few crumbs of love. Once his neediness is satisfied, he becomes more discerning. It is as though he wakes up from the dream of infatuation and is suddenly no longer interested. It is already hard enough for men to commit these days; getting involved on the rebound just compounds the problem.

A man on the rebound can
fall in love with almost anyone who
offers him a few crumbs of love.

After a relationship ends, a man may feel like a failure. To prove his manhood or his competence as a man, he will seek out a sexual partner and "score." While this may make him feel good, it is also an excellent opportunity to heal the feelings that come up automatically. A woman's love can make him feel good about himself and support his healing process. But he must be careful to not make promises. When a relationship ends, a man needs to take time to free himself from making a commitment. A man's strength and success in the future is based on his ability to feel good about himself without depending on the security of a committed relationship.

GETTING INVOLVED AT THE RIGHT TIME

The time for a man to begin a relationship is when his desire to give is greater than his need to receive. It weakens a man to get in a relationship in which he receives more than he gives. It just makes him more needy and self-absorbed. He must be careful that when he gets involved, he does so from a place of power. He must feel that he has the power to provide for a woman's happiness, not just that she has the power to fulfill him. When a man has sex before he is ready for a commitment, he must make his intentions clear, that he is on the rebound and seeks the comfort of a woman's love and is not ready for a commitment.

It weakens a man to get in a
relationship where he receives
more than he gives.

The woman, however, is generally the one who feels the hurt of this mistake more than the man. This wounded man shows up in her life showering her with the warmth of his appreciation, gratitude, and love, and then pulls it all back. One day his feelings have suddenly changed for no apparent reason. Although she has not changed, his feelings have. No longer fueled by the hunger of deprivation, he doesn't really need or appreciate her at all. Although he came on really strong, he loses interest just as quickly. This pattern is obviously not nurturing for her, nor is it good for him.

A wise woman is careful only to have sex with a man on the rebound if she has no expectations of a lasting commitment. She must be prepared for him to stop calling at any time. If she chooses to have sex she must recognize that his feelings are temporary. Then she will not be hurt. Without this insight, when he breaks up with her, she has to deal with the hurt and sense of betrayal and he has to deal with feelings of guilt. To avoid feeling his guilt, he suppresses his negative feelings by getting into another relationship. This pattern will continue indefinitely until he stops and takes the required time to heal his pain. Unless he abstains from making promises on the rebound, he will never find lasting love.

RECOGNIZING THE RIGHT PERSON

Unresolved feelings of hurt and guilt prevent us from being able to see or recognize the right person for us. Getting involved on the rebound almost insures that we will get involved with the wrong person. The more guilt a man feels (or suppresses) from disappointing a woman, the longer he will have to wait before he is able to recognize the right woman for him.

Getting involved on the rebound
almost insures that we will get involved
with the wrong person.

When a man gets involved with a woman from a position of weakness and neediness, he will almost always seek a new woman when he begins to feel his strength and independence. From his new position of power, he will want a woman he can provide for, not a mother to take care of him.

He will want a woman who sees and appreciates his strength, not his weakness. It doesn't matter if a woman has sacrificed herself for him or given him the best years of her life. If she is not right for him, he will need to move on. No matter what she has given him, it cannot make her the right woman for him. A man can only sustain attraction for a woman when she is the right woman for him. In most cases, the woman a man picks on the rebound is not the right woman for him. Nor is he the right man for her.

It could also be that a woman is right for a man, but he cannot see it or feel it. Getting involved on the rebound may actually prevent him from recognizing her as a suitable partner. If she was there for him when he was down, when he goes up, they will both feel that he owes her. This sense of debt and obligation may prevent him from feeling his love for her. The grass will seem much greener on the other side of the fence.

Getting involved on the rebound may
actually prevent a man from recognizing
his partner as a suitable partner.

The sense of owing someone prevents a man from freely choosing to be in a relationship. When he feels he *should* be with her because he owes her, he is often not able to be with her. His debt to her is like a ball and chain around his ankle. The thought of getting involved with a new partner is like getting out of prison without any record. Starting over with a clean slate is very tempting.

2

SEX ON THE REBOUND

One of the biggest obstacles for men in the process of healing their hearts is their hunger for sex. It is very easy for a man to confuse his need for love with his need for sex. Although he may sense that he is not ready to get involved emotionally, he wants to get involved sexually. Although this casual sexual involvement will provide temporary relief, it is not healing. After each sexual encounter, he needs to take time to explore the feelings that come up.

Sex is a beautiful expression of love and intimacy. When our hearts are wounded, sex becomes a potent means for a man to connect with his feelings. Yet he must be careful to not commit himself, for it reinforces his dependency on a woman's love at this time. It is best for him to be sexually involved with a series of partners, or at least make it clear that he is not capable of making any promises.

A persistent hunger for sex on the rebound

could turn into an addiction. After finding temporary relief, he must then process his pain. He may
avoid his healing feelings by rushing into more
sex. If we are not careful, sexual stimulation may
become a means to avoid and numb our feelings
instead of being a means to connect with and
comfort our pain.

By temporarily abstaining from sexual stimulation, a man has a greater chance of completing the
healing process. If this is very difficult for him,
then it is a sign that he needs to do it. He can
make it much easier for himself by avoiding circumstances that will overstimulate him.

By temporarily abstaining from sexual
stimulation, a man has a greater chance
of completing the healing process.

If he is using more sex to avoid his feelings, this
is not the time to watch X-rated videos, read
pornographic magazines, or cruise around looking for a woman. This kind of sexual stimulation
will only reinforce his need for sex. Cold showers,
exercise, and time spent with friends are the best
ways to maintain sexual control.

ADDICTIONS ARE NOT REAL NEEDS

Addictions feel like real needs, but they are not.
They are actually *replacement* needs. When it is
too painful to feel a real need, the mind creates a
new need, a replacement need. A man's obsessive

hunger for sex on the rebound is a replacement need. His real need is the need to heal his feelings: sex in moderation will help him get in touch, but obsessive sex can obstruct the healing process.

Men are more prone to addictions than women, because they are generally less adept at the process of sharing their feelings. Most men do not have friendships or communication skills that can nurture a more in-depth conversation about intimate feelings. To cope with the normal stress of living, men generally talk with each other about sports, business, politics, and the weather. This is generally good enough until a man's heart is broken.

Men generally talk about sports, business, politics, and the weather, not painful and vulnerable feelings.

After the loss of love, if a man does not know where to turn, often he succumbs to addictive tendencies. His real need to share his feelings gets replaced by a false need. This same principle is true for women as well. Men are more inclined to feel a sexual addiction, while women are more vulnerable to overeating as an addiction. Unless we clearly understand and apply the insights of healing our hearts, then we may be gripped by the seductive pull of our addictive tendencies.

3

POSITIVE ADDICTIONS

During a healing crisis, if a man does not recognize his ability to create opportunities to share his feelings, he suffers. To escape this suffering, he seeks relief through addictions. The most common of all addictions for men is sex, then come destructive addictions like alcohol and drugs. Any behavior when performed in excess can be used as a means to suppress feelings.

To escape our suffering,
we seek relief through addictions.

Men commonly become addicted to their work during a healing crisis. Although overworking can be an addiction, it is less of an obstacle to the healing process. It is a more positive addiction. It can actually help facilitate a man's process of healing. If a man is also getting support in counseling or from a group, focusing on his work can bring him a good deal of healthy relief. His work becomes a way for him to feel independent and autonomous again and not so dependent on an intimate love relationship.

While it is healthy for men to focus on their work during a healing crisis, it is not so healthy for women. A woman has a tendency to avoid her own feelings by giving too much of herself. By focusing on her work or giving to others, a woman may become overly responsible for others and as a result repress her own feelings and needs. A woman should be careful that she doesn't lose herself in her work.

For men, work can be a positive addiction, but for women it can obstruct the healing process.

Honest work helps a man heal his heart. As he succeeds in giving to others, the appreciation, acceptance, and trust that others give him actually gives him the strength and ability to look more deeply into his feelings and heal them. During a healing crisis, anything a man does to be helpful of others or to be more independent and autonomous will facilitate his inner process of healing.

Recreation can also be a positive addiction. It is very good for him to get out and do things that make him feel good. This is the time when he should do special things for himself as well. If he has been wanting a new car, this is the time to buy it. If he wants a new stereo, this is the time to go shopping. Certainly having fun or spending too much could be addictions, but in moderation they are positive addictions. As long as a man has the money to spend, this is the time to spend it. As long as his children are getting what they need and he is being responsible in satisfying his work requirements, this is the best time of his life to take time off and have fun. This is the time to do the things he couldn't do when he was married.

4

WORK, MONEY, AND LOVE

It is still possible for a man to bury himself so much in his work that he ignores his feelings of loss. To the extent that he suppresses his feelings of sorrow and powerlessness, he may create situations at work that are impossible to solve. He will take on more than he can do and then feel powerless to achieve his goals.

If a past partner demanded too much, and he doesn't deal with his anger, he may begin to require too much from himself. His suppressed anger will actually cause him to become like his former demanding partner. He sets unrealistic and demanding goals that require all of his time and energy.

A man should be careful to set realistic goals for himself. Otherwise he will create enormous pressure to measure up to his own unrealistic standards. This pressure to work harder gives him even fewer opportunities to heal the very hurt that is fueling his unhealthy obsession.

> A man creates enormous pressure
> to measure up to his own
> unrealistic standards.

One successful businessman I know resolved, after a painful breakup, that he would not get involved again until he had made ten million dollars. This kind of pressure is not healthy. After healing from a breakup, ideally a man should not feel that he has to achieve anything more than he already has.

He should not have to do more in order to have a loving relationship. The right woman for him will not love him for his money, but because he is right for her.

> By setting financial goals as a
> prerequisite for a relationship,
> a man is placing too much
> importance on money.

After being in a negative and unsupportive relationship, a man may also conclude that to get ahead he will do better without a partner. While certainly it is ideal that a man be able to take care of his own needs before getting into an intimate partnership, he doesn't have to wait until he has "made it."

By creating a balance between love and work, a man's chances of finding success and then keeping that success go up dramatically. The foundation of a loving relationship assists a man greatly in being able to accomplish his goals.

In my own life, I used to feel that I had to be hugely successful to be worthy of love. It's not as if I walked around thinking, I have to be more successful or I will not be loved. In my conscious mind, I just felt a huge pressure to be successful. I was never quite satisfied with what I had achieved. Whatever I did, it was never enough.

A man's pressure to achieve is often fueled by the incorrect notion that to be loved he must be more successful.

What fueled this pressure, however, was the subconscious feeling that I had to have more in order to be loved. As long as I thought that way, not only was I less successful, but I was never satisfied. When I married my wife Bonnie, that all changed.

Within a couple of years, I experienced the healing power of love. As she continued to love me, I experienced that I didn't need to do more or have more to get her love. What she loved most was the time we spent together. This changed my whole perspective about work.

While starting over, instead of working harder and longer hours, try working a little less and focusing more on your needs for friendship and recreation. Not only will you find the support to heal your heart, but you will attract more success.

In my own life, as I learned to balance my emotional needs with my work needs, my success increased. That success has just continued to increase. Each day I have opportunities that tempt me once more to overwork, but I restrain myself by remembering the basis of my success. By watering the root of my success, like a plant, it will continue to flourish.

When a man works to keep his heart open, he is tending to the basis of his success at work. When he is loved and trusted by his friends and family, the world trusts him as well. A balanced life is like a magnet that will draw in opportunities for greater success.

5

LOVE IS NOT ENOUGH

Men and woman make the mistake of assuming that love is enough to make a relationship last. Sometimes two people love each other, but they are not right for each other. They may love each other a lot, but not enough to be married or stay married. Commonly in our society we hold the notion that if we love someone, we should get married. If we love someone, then he/she is the one. Though certainly love is a prerequisite for a lasting and fulfilling relationship, love does not guarantee that a person is right for us.

Picking a mate is similar to picking a job. There are many jobs that we could do, but we must search within our soul to find the right job for us. We can love to do a lot of things, but in the end we must focus in one direction. In a similar way, there can be thousands of people we could love, but only a few could be marriage partners. From that small group we must search our soul to discover who is right for us.

When we try to make each other right, we end up creating problems. We either change ourselves too much to fulfill our partner's needs, or they try to change themselves too much. For a marriage to succeed, we need to feel we can be more of ourselves and not less. If one partner has to give up who they are to make the other happy, it cannot work.

No matter how much you love someone, you cannot put a square peg in a round hole.

In trying to stay together, we may spiral downward until we stop liking each other. In truth we have just stopped liking who we have become. Part of staying in love is liking the person we become while relating with our partner. Each relationship we have brings out a part of who we are. The right person will bring out the best in us. When a partner is not the right person to be intimately involved with, she can bring out the worst in us. Instead of becoming more loving, wise, receptive, and creative, we stop growing.

Ironically, when two people who love each other are able to end their relationship with forgiveness, understanding that they just were not right for each other, they are able to be very good friends as long as they do not try to sustain an intimate romantic relationship.

Without understanding that sometimes it is

impossible to make a relationship work, one or both partners may remain stuck. At the end of the relationship, one partner or both may feel guilty because they were not able to make it work. To avoid feeling this guilt, a person may stay in a relationship long after he realizes it is time to go. Only after things get worse and worse do we feel justified in leaving. Unfortunately, the longer we stay, the more we have disappointed or even hurt each other. And so there is more guilt to heal and release.

To avoid feelings of guilt, a person
may stay in a relationship long
after he realizes it is time to go.

Recognizing that two people can love each other but not be able to make an intimate relationship work is the basis of letting go without guilt and letting go with forgiveness. With this insight we can still say, "I love you; we are just not right for each other." We can acknowledge that we did our best but we were not right for each other. We can acknowledge that our partner did her best as well. By keeping our heart open in this way, our chances of picking the right partner next time dramatically goes up.

When we look for a new relationship feeling bad, guilty, inadequate, or like a failure, it is much more difficult to find the right person. On the other hand, ending a relationship with love while recognizing that our partner was not right automatically points us in the right direction to find a more suitable mate for us. Feelings of guilt are a sign that we need more healing before we are ready to move on.

6

LEARNING FROM
OUR MISTAKES

One of the ways a man suppresses his feelings of loss is by blaming his ex-partner. By simply recognizing that she was the wrong woman for him, he can easily dismiss and suppress his natural feelings of loss. He reasons that it was a good thing that they parted ways. This rationalization discounts any feelings of loss.

Not only does this prevent him from opening his heart again, but it prevents him from looking at how he contributed to the problems of a relationship. The problems of a relationship are never one person's fault. It is not enough simply to say, "I got involved with the wrong person."

A part of being able to find the right
person in the future is learning from
our mistakes in previous relationships.

When two people who are not right for each other come together and try to make a relationship work, they will inevitably bring out the worst in each other. Being with the right person doesn't magically make all the problems go away, either.

Whether we are with the right person or the wrong person, we contribute to our problems. To make sure that we don't repeat our patterns, when we end a relationship we need to be accountable for how we contributed to the problems. By looking at the ways we contributed to the problems of our last relationship, we can make sure that we are more loving in future relationships.

When we learn from our past, we are more capable of creating what we want in the future. To blame all our problems on our ex-partner is missing an important opportunity to learn and grow. Not only will we continue to make the same mistakes, but we will automatically be attracted to the same kind of partner.

When we learn from our past,
then we are more capable of creating
what we want in the future.

It is easy for a man to forget, but not as easy to forgive. When he is involved in another relationship and similar issues begin to come up, instead of dealing with them freshly, he will tend to be less tolerant. Before moving on it is very helpful for a man to explore not only the mistakes and misgivings of his partner, but also his mistakes in the relationship. By taking time to review his behavior he will be forgiving and not merely forgetting what happened.

7

WE DON'T HAVE TO
STOP LOVING

Although a man has recognized that his ex-partner is not the right partner for him, it doesn't mean he has to stop loving her. Often a man will feel that he has to stop loving his partner in order to say good-bye. He doesn't realize that he can say, "I love you and I realize that we are not right for each other. We will do better as friends." Certainly his love for her may have changed, but he does not have to close his heart in order to leave a relationship.

When we leave a relationship, we need to take time to remember the love we shared in the beginning. This is a very important part of resetting a broken heart.

8

UNREQUITED LOVE

Men tend to be motivated by challenge. When we want something and it is not easily attained, we want it more. For a man, challenge creates passion. When we want a woman's love, are attracted to her love, and can't have it, then the flames of our passion may dramatically increase.

When a relationship ends, sometimes a man will pine away in agony for the woman he loves. He cannot believe that she doesn't want him. This only makes him want her more and fuels the unbearable pain of separation. This feeling of unrequited love helps him to find his feelings of sorrow, but there are other feelings he needs to explore as well.

When a man experiences the pain of unrequited love, the pain of star-crossed lovers who cannot find each other or consummate their relationship, it is clearly an indicator that he has unresolved feelings from his past. This tendency not to accept rejection or to be hurt by the loss of love began much earlier in his life.

> The agonizing pain of star-crossed
> lovers clearly indicates unresolved
> feelings from the past.

To free himself from the passionate and agonizing grip of unrequited love, a man needs to link his pain in the present with his past. He needs to search in his memory for other situations when he first started dating and then earlier to a time when he felt rejected or abandoned in some way by his mother.

For a man, the inability to let go is often linked to unresolved feelings regarding his mother's love. As a child, if he was rushed to let go of needing his mother before he was ready to let go, then a part of him is still holding on. It could be that his mother died when he was young, or that for some time they were very close and then another child came along. By linking his painful feelings in the present with his past, he can begin to free himself from their grip.

It is perfectly normal for him to feel that no woman will ever measure up and that he will never find happiness. These are the kind of thoughts that fuel the pain and drama of unrequited love. If we were able to see into the future and know that we will find an even better love, then we would not be so upset.

Since we can't know the future, we remain in our pain. If we process a past situation of unrequited love, then we know from the vantage point of the present that we will find a greater love. In listening to our past feelings from the present, we can enrich the exploration of our past pain with this reassuring insight.

9

TAKING RESPONSIBILITY TO LET GO

Sometimes a man can't move on because he doesn't take responsibility to let go. He feels she has left him, but he holds on to the idea that she is wrong. Blaming her in this way prevents him from moving on to feeling good again. Ideally, when a relationship ends it is a mutual decision. Then one person doesn't end up feeling like a victim.

At some point, he must decide within himself that they really were not right for each other. Maybe they could have made it work if circumstances and timing were different. From this more positive perspective, he can be more forgiving and be open to creating a new and wonderful life for himself.

When a man feels as if he has been left and he still wants his partner, he can easily get stuck in blame and judgment. If he has children, he can make another big mistake by talking about their mother as if she were selfish and not caring about anyone. He needs to keep these kinds of feelings to himself and his therapist.

As parents we should always be very careful not to harshly judge or criticize the other parent in front of our children. It is very difficult for them. It creates all kinds of problems when a child is forced to side with one parent against the other parent.

If a man feels he loves his partner and she should not have left him, then it is up to him to model what real love is. If he really loves his partner, then he should support her in doing what she feels is right for her. It is wrong for him to treat her as if she is his child or property. This is not love. If he really wants her to come back, then the best approach is to let go.

HANDLING REJECTION

It cannot hold true that someone is right for us, but we are not right for them. If a woman does not want us, then clearly she is not the right person for us. To believe otherwise is to remain a victim and to hold on to our hurt and loss.

To let go we must recognize that she might have been close to the right woman for us, but she was not the one.

It does not serve us to idealize a woman who does not want us. From this perspective we can see that the following thoughts are logically inconsistent:

> "We were perfect together, if only I had not made that mistake."
>
> "We are perfect together, if only she would move out here to be with me."
>
> "We should be together, if only she hadn't met that other guy."
>
> "We could be perfect for each other, if only I had met her sooner."
>
> "We would be perfect together, if only she were not already taken."

If she really were perfect for you, then she would forgive your mistake, she would move out to be with you, you would have met her at the right time, she wouldn't be in love with another guy, she would be available and not already taken . . . If we are to hold the idea that someone is perfect for us, then we need to define perfection correctly at least as being available to us.

It is the illusion of infatuation to believe that someone who does not love, accept, or want us could possibly be the right person for us.

To let go of a woman who does not want him, a man must recognize that she doesn't want him. This acknowledgment is painful, but it helps a man to face and to endure the truth that she does not love him enough to stay with him. She does not want to be with him. While this general acknowledgment is important, it is not helpful to focus on the specific reasons for her not wanting him.

Focusing on the specific reasons, she might say he is not rich enough, not smart enough, not sophisticated enough, too complicated, too selfish, too driven, too incentive-oriented, etc. These are just superficial conditions. The real reason she doesn't want him is that he is not right for her. If he were right for her, then these things would not matter. Focusing on these kinds of conditions, a man can easily get caught up thinking, But I can change . . . This takes him down the wrong road.

A COMPLETION PROCESS

If a couple is in counseling together at the end of their relationship, this completion process can be very helpful. The counselor asks her, as a way to help him let go, to repeat the following phrases again and again. Directly feeling the pain of his loss will eventually help him to let go. She simply says over and over to him the following phrases:

"I don't want to be with you."
"I don't love you as much as I thought."
"You are not the right partner for me."
"I want to be with someone else."
"I will always love you, but not enough to
    stay with you."
"I know you are not the right person for me."

By hearing these phrases over and over, he will get a chance clearly to experience the break and to let go. After doing this exercise, the therapist should ask the woman to leave the room and take some time to explore the four healing emotions with her partner.

To complete the exercise, he should say the same phrases to her. Even if he doesn't fully feel it yet, he should just do it. By saying the words, he gets a chance to experience the truth, which has a chance to take hold and free him from the illusory grip of his pain.

If she is not in counseling with him, then he can role-play this same exercise with a therapist. The therapist becomes his ex-partner and repeats these rejecting but honest expressions. The man then has a chance to feel and process the feelings that come up in response. After taking time to explore the feelings that come up, he can complete the exercise by expressing these same statements in return.

10

SOUL MATES ARE NOT PERFECT

Sometimes a man will be unable to make a commitment because he compares his new partner to some perfect fantasy woman of his dreams. He may love a woman, but wonder if he is making the right decision to be with her. He wants to make sure he gets the best woman he can. He worries that maybe somewhere there is a better woman. By expecting his soul mate to be perfect, he does not give himself a chance to find true and lasting love.

This man postpones making a commitment because he is expecting perfection. He imagines that his soul mate is perfect. He does not have a realistic perspective of relationships and people. A soul mate is not a perfect person. There is no such person. A soul mate is perfect for him.

A soul mate is not perfect,
but perfect for us.

The realization that a woman is a man's soul mate happens after he takes time to get to know her. It is unrealistic to expect this recognition right away. It takes time for our hearts to open fully to one another. When love grows, then we just know one day if our partner is right for us. This recognition is not a mental assessment. It is a natural knowing.

The right person for us is recognized by our souls, not by our mind. The soul does not figure things out. It just knows "This is the person for me." If we try to figure out if a partner is right, then we will be judging her from our mind. From this perspective, she will never be enough. Our mind will always find a list of flaws. To pick a soul mate, we must choose from our soul.

You cannot pick a soul mate by trying
to figure out if she is right.

Ideally we should use our minds to figure out how we can most effectively give and receive love and support. As we succeed in the dating process by using our minds, our hearts begin to open. With an open heart, our soul can then guide us to continue on or to break up.

Sometimes when our hearts open, we discover that our partner is not right for us. As we have already discussed, love is not enough. Just because we love our partner does not mean that she is right for us. A soul mate is someone with whom in our heart of hearts we feel a longing to share our lives. We may love someone, but not want to share our lives with her.

11

BEING IN A HURRY

A man may miss the opportunity to love by being in a hurry. He is a man with a mission. If he doesn't know for sure if a woman is the right one, he will just move on. He doesn't want to get more involved because he doesn't want to waste time. Time is precious. He reasons that by spending too much time in one relationship, he may be missing the opportunity to find the right woman.

With greater insight regarding the process of finding a soul mate, he can relax and take his time. If he loves a woman but doesn't know for sure if she is the right one, he is not wasting his time.

By continuing the relationship until he knows for sure either way, he is preparing himself to find his soul mate.

If he continues to love his partner, but later discovers she is not the one, he has not lost time. He has wisely spent that time opening his heart and developing his ability to know and recognize a soul mate. By taking time to grieve the end of his relationship, his chances of finding the right person next time dramatically go up.

Although he has struck out, his time has not been wasted. Next time his chances of hitting a home run go up dramatically. Babe Ruth was the home run record holder, but he also held the record for the most strikeouts. By giving his all, he would strike out more often, but soon after he would hit a home run.

12

RECOGNIZING A SOUL MATE

We often worry too much about picking the right partner. Although each woman is unique and special, what we can receive in any relationship has more to do with what we give than the person we are giving to. If a man could be with many women, what he would get back would be very similar in almost every case. When our soul recognizes a mate, we are not recognizing a woman who is better than the others. We are recognizing someone with whom we can grow together in love for a lifetime.

> What we get out of a relationship has
> more to do with what we give than
> who the person is.

When we recognize our soul mate, it feels as if we have found the one person with whom we are to share our lives. Because it is our soul's choice, it feels as though it was meant to be. Although recognizing our soul mate feels like destiny, it is still a choice. It is too limiting to think that there could only be one person for us. This kind of thinking would make anyone nervous about making a choice.

It is too limiting to think that there
could only be one person for us.

A man will often make the mistake of thinking there is one perfect woman who is better than all the rest. This makes it very difficult to decide, because there is no such woman. For any one man, there could be hundreds of women whom he could pick. Often men will say to me, "How do I pick one? They are all so wonderful! There are so many, and each is so different."

The answer to this question is that you don't decide in your mind. You just pick one that seems as good as the rest and you give the relationship a chance. If you grow in love, as you give to the relationship, then your heart can open more fully. When the heart is open, you gain the ability to know if this one is right for you. If she is not the one, then next time you will get closer to finding the one for you.

13

LIVING OUT OUR FANTASIES

When a man is ready to start over, often he will only pursue the women who fit his "picture." Every man walks around with a picture in his mind of the ideal woman for him. Most of the time, the woman who turns out to be the perfect partner for him doesn't fit his picture at all. She is a complete surprise.

When men only pursue women who fit their picture, they postpone their chances of finding the right woman. Quite often a man will go to a party and be turned on by a variety of women. However, he will ignore his feelings of attraction simply because a woman does not look the way he thinks she should look.

A man will ignore his feelings of attraction unless a woman looks a certain way.

If a man can just put away his pictures for a while and date the women to whom he is attracted, he would have a much better chance of finding the right person. Instead of focusing on what a woman looks like, it is better for a man to focus on how she makes him feel.

Physical attraction disappears very quickly. Passion can only be sustained when the attraction we feel is based on something more than just a woman's physical appearance. A soul mate is someone we feel attracted to on all four levels of our being: physical, emotional, mental, and spiritual. We are sexually attracted to her, we like her, we find her interesting, and we are inspired by her to be the most we can be. To experience a lifetime of love and not just a few weeks, months, or years, we must connect on all four levels.

Passion can only be sustained
when the attraction we feel is
based on something more than
just her physical appearance.

I was surprised when female clients who looked like movie stars and models would almost always complain that their boyfriends or husbands were no longer attracted to them. If they were not involved, they were often very disappointed by the many men who wanted them, but then quickly lost interest. This was not because they were unlovable in any way, but because they had gotten involved with the wrong men. They were involved with men who were only attracted from the physical level.

If we want to be happy and well loved for a lifetime, the wise man doesn't judge a book by its cover. Some men still have difficulty with this approach. They can't bear to give up the hope that they can find the perfect woman who looks like a centerfold. Yet, when they get her, there is always some flaw that begins to stand out. Focusing too much on the physical will never be satisfying for long. The following analysis can assist a man to let go of his picture:

When a man looks at an attractive woman, what makes her so wonderful? She is so beautiful. She is truly awesome to behold. Because of this, she makes him feel really good. She turns him on. She makes him want to touch her, and when he does it feels so good. To touch her excites him and excites her.

This reflection demonstrates that what makes a man happiest is how a woman makes him feel. A man's primary requirement should be how she makes him feel when he looks at her, not just how she looks.

Sometimes a man will hold on to his fantasies for the same reason he will cling to a past partner. He is attached. As we have previously discussed, to let go of his attachments he must fully grieve his loss. If a man is attached to a picture, it clearly indicates that somewhere in his past relationships he has not yet let go.

14

CAN'T LIVE WITH THEM AND CAN'T LIVE WITHOUT THEM

After a string of failed relationships, some men just give up. They stop trying. They seek the companionship of women, but when the problems begin to come up they just move on. Instead of learning from their experiences, they form limiting and negative generalizations. These men don't have a positive perspective to understand how men and women are different. They love women, but they have concluded that they can't live with them. They are willing to get involved, but not interested in getting married.

These men have incorrect expectations of the way a woman should respond to situations. When she doesn't respond the way he would, he experiences tremendous frustration. He judges her and tries to change her, rather than consider changing his approach. Frustration between men and women particularly occurs in the area of communication.

She wants to talk when he doesn't. He wants his space, and she wants together time. She wants him to listen, but when he gives his solutions, she disregards his advice, and he feels unappreciated. He does his best, but it never seems to be enough for her. It is hard for love to grow when we are always butting heads.

When a man gives solutions to a woman she may become even more frustrated.

When a man continues to experience the same issues again and again, instead of concluding that something is wrong with women, he needs to look at how he is contributing to the problems. Often by making a few adjustments in his approach, he can experience exactly what he wants and hopes for in a loving relationship. By taking time to learn about the different ways men and women communicate, he can change this pattern.

Sometimes this issue is deeper than just what he understands about the opposite sex. If a man's feelings remain unresolved from a past relationship, he may never feel any woman is good enough. As soon as he begins to get close to a woman and feel his natural love and devotion, some hurt part of him comes up and says, "Hold it, I've done this before and it didn't work; I ended up feeling like a fool. This can hurt . . ."

If a man's feelings remain unresolved,
he may never feel any woman
is good enough.

Deep inside, if some part of a man feels hurt, rejected, or inadequate, as he gets closer to a woman these feelings will begin to surface. When they arise they don't identify themselves as past feelings. Instead, a man may feel that something is wrong with his partner. When men feel inadequate, they are quick to defend themselves by blaming another.

If a man feels unworthy, it is hard for him to value someone who would value him. This attitude is like the joke, "I wouldn't want to belong to any club that would have me as a member." When a woman easily surrenders to a man's advances, he may begin to question how much he wants her or how much he wants the relationship. Then when issues come up, he has a difficult time valuing the relationship enough to get through the tough times.

15

THE ENDLESS SEARCH

Some men are always looking. They are never content with one woman, but endlessly search for the right one. They continue to push love away by assuming that out there somewhere is a woman who will not be difficult. When he experiences the normal challenges that come up in almost every relationship, he naively concludes that he is with the wrong partner. He mistakenly assumes that he keeps getting the lemons.

It is naive to expect always to get along in a relationship or always to get everything you want. Every relationship has its up moments and its down moments. In a good relationship, couples work through their challenges and end up getting closer. They are able to look back and laugh about their frustrations and disappointments.

Without a realistic expectation of the way relationships work, a man will eventually conclude that there is nothing he can do to make it work. When his partner complains about something, if he doesn't get the kind of response he wants, after he has expressed his point of view, he quickly gives up. Although, to her, it seems as if he doesn't care, it is really that he doesn't know what to do.

When a man senses that he can solve a problem, then he will feel the energy to stay with it until it is done. If he concludes that he doesn't know what to do, then he gives up. For example, if something goes wrong with his computer, he will spend long hours tending to it. The difference between the computer and his partner is that he knows computers are supposed to have problems and he assumes that by looking at his manuals and changing the settings he will eventually succeed. This expectation of success fuels his interest and staying power.

WOMEN'S ISSUES AND COMPLAINTS

If a man mistakenly concludes that he is just picking the wrong women, then he will have little interest in trying to solve the problems and issues that come up. A man sabotages his chances of finding lasting love by not expecting relationships to have problems and difficulties at times. What man would assume that his work should always be easy and fun? Life is a balance of work and play. It is naive to expect a relationship to be any different.

A man sabotages his chances
of finding love by expecting
relationships to be problem free.

After counseling thousands of men and women, I came to the very clear conclusion that women in general have pretty much the same complaints and issues with men. As they spoke with me, they thought that their problems were unique to their relationship. They had no idea that all week, every week, I would hear the same stories.

While each relationship is certainly unique and special, there are many patterns, issues, complaints, and misunderstandings that occur in almost every intimate relationship. After reading *Men Are from Mars, Women Are from Venus*, men and women will commonly tell me that I must have been hiding under their beds and listening to their conversations. They feel a certain relief to know that they are not alone and other people experience what they experience. A part of their relief is also the recognition that "if other people are experiencing this, then I am not missing out."

The man on the endless search feels he is missing out in some way. With this new insight he can finally relax. Regardless of who he picks, he will eventually get the same kinds of responses he has always gotten. He will never find a woman who is not a woman.

This does not mean that he cannot get what he needs from a relationship; instead, it gives him an opportunity to find real love. It is easy to love perfection. Real love is learning to love a real person with all her flaws and differences.

Regardless of who a man picks, he will
eventually get the same kinds of
responses he has always gotten.

He has not been getting "lemons." He just
didn't know how to sweeten a lemon and make
lemonade. He mistakenly concluded that his difficulties had to do with picking the wrong woman.
Now he can be comforted with the knowledge
that whatever woman he finds, he will have to
deal with the same kinds of issues. On the foundation that certain issues are inevitable, he can
begin to recognize that the frustration he experiences has more to do with his approach than the
woman he picks.

Women also benefit greatly from this insight.
Although a woman is more inclined to recognize
that relationships have difficulties, she will often
resist a man's unique tendencies. Often women
have told me that recognizing the ways men are
different has helped them to accept their husbands
instead of trying to change them. Often, a woman
takes it very personally when a man reacts differently or neglects to do something she would
remember to do. With an understanding of how
men are different, she can laugh instead and realize he's from Mars.

16

HOLDING BACK

If a man does not take the time to grieve his loss, he may unknowingly push away the opportunity to love by holding back. When it is time for him to begin dating again, if he has not taken the necessary time to release his negative feelings and forgive his past partner, he will hold back from making a commitment.

Right after a breakup, pulling back is very healthy. Before getting involved, it is important for a man to regain once more his sense of independence, self-sufficiency, and autonomy. If he doesn't take enough time to hold back from making a commitment, then once he does get involved, he will inevitably break his commitment.

If he has failed to please his partner in the past, instead of risking the possibility of getting burned again, he doesn't try so hard. He takes the attitude that he wants to be loved for who he is and not what he does. He is overly careful not to give too much of himself or make any promises.

This kind of holding back is not productive for a man. If he is going to get involved, then he should be prepared to do and give his best. A helpful motto from Mars is "If a job is worth doing, then it is worth doing your best." If he doesn't do his best, then he loses.

If a job is worth doing, then
it is worth doing your best.

A man thrives when he feels that he is successful in being there for others. His self-esteem comes from doing things for others and feeling successful. He grows through making promises and doing his best to keep them. When his efforts in the past have not been appreciated, the fault lies not in his intention to please and provide for others but in the lack of appreciation he received. If a man has not been appreciated, instead of holding back from giving, he needs to give to someone who will appreciate him.

A man's greatest challenge is to put his best foot forward when his efforts have not been appreciated in the past. He may try again, but he still holds back from doing his best. He holds back to protect himself. In case he fails, there is some comfort in saying to himself, "Well, I didn't really try." What he doesn't realize is that by holding back he disconnects from his inner strength and power.

MEN HOLD BACK, WOMEN GIVE TOO MUCH

While starting over, unless we first heal our hearts, a man tends to hold back while a woman will tend to give too much. Women have a special need to feel loved just the way they are without having to earn it. Certainly a woman enjoys doing things for others and being appreciated, but her sense of worth hinges on being loved without having to be there for others. A woman *primarily* needs to be loved for who she is rather than for what she does. When she depends too much on being loved for her doing, she tends to over-give.

A woman *primarily* needs
to be loved for who she is rather
than for what she does.

Certainly both men and women should be loved for who they are and not just for what they bring to a relationship. But men also have a special need. They *primarily* need to be appreciated for what they do. If a man is just loved for who he is, it will never be enough for him. Something will be missing. To fully receive love, a man needs to experience that the love he receives is the result of his efforts and achievement, not just because he is a good and loving person.

A man feels best about himself when his actions can nurture the needs of others. If in past relationships a man's actions have not been enough, then until that pain is healed he will hold back. Unless he is able to forgive his past partner, he will be limited in what he can freely give in the future. Before he makes a commitment again, he must make sure he is ready to put his best foot forward and not hold back.

17

BEING VS. DOING

A man can easily become confused and give up wanting to please a woman. He may claim defiantly that he wants to be loved for who he is and not what he does. He doesn't want to be a slave anymore, working day in and day out to provide for a woman. He begins to feel he is a working machine whose worth is measured by his output. He wants to be loved for his being and not his doing.

While all of these sentiments are valid, they are the symptoms of unhealed hurt. They are a man's reactions to not feeling appreciated for what he can do or has done. This man has given up trying to please a woman because he feels his past efforts have been for naught. He feels his efforts were not recognized, so why bother again?

Instead of giving up his intention to please a woman, a man needs to learn how to be successful in pleasing a woman. To accomplish this, his challenge is twofold. First, he needs to recognize that he can want to please a woman, but not feel responsible for her happiness. Second, he needs to reconsider what works and what doesn't. Instead of giving up completely, he can wisely give up just those actions that don't work.

A man needs to recognize that he can seek to please a woman without taking responsibility for her happiness.

When a man feels overly responsible for a woman's happiness, then when she is not happy he feels beaten up. When she is unhappy, he feels like a failure. Ideally, a man should not feel responsible for a woman's happiness. A wise man knows that a woman is responsible for how she feels. He is only responsible at unhappy times to help. He cannot do it for her. If he takes on too much responsibility, then it will feel like he has been beaten over the head with a big stick.

There is a world of difference between doing your best to make a woman happy and doing your best and then requiring her to be happy right away. To understand a woman, a man needs to recognize that sometimes the way to make her happy is to empathize with her when she is unhappy. When a woman feels bad or unhappy, the last thing she wants is some man trying to solve her problems to make her feel good. Instead of a solution, she wants to feel what she feels for a while and to have him understand what she is going through.

When a man feels overly responsible for a woman's happiness, he feels beaten up when she is not happy.

Instead of not helping at all, a man needs to realize that sometimes the best way to help is just to be there for her. In this case, *being there* is actually doing something for her. With a deeper understanding of the way women think and feel, a man can actually be much more successful in his relationship. He can freely give his support without having to feel responsible for how she feels.

He can actually give less and be more supportive. When a man gives too much, he ends up feeling too dependent on the outcome. By giving in the right measure, he doesn't have to hold back from giving, but instead gives what he can and gets the appreciation that he needs.

18

BIGGER IS BETTER

Ideally, a man should not feel that his worth is measured by his output. He shouldn't be a slave to his work or feel pressured to perform and provide in order to be loved. He should work and provide because he wants to work. The pressure he feels has more to do with himself than with a woman's desire to be pleased. He may feel that to be loved and appreciated he has to do more than he can do or is doing.

In most cases, when a man resists identifying himself as a provider, he is expecting too much of himself. Instead of recognizing that what he can do is worthy of love, he mistakenly succumbs to the pressure from society that he has to do more, accomplish more, and have more to be worthy of a woman's love. He gets caught up in the belief that bigger is better.

While counseling couples, I have repeatedly found that what men need most is to release their focus on doing the big things and focus more on the little things. It is action that sweeps a woman off her feet, but she is not dependent on a man's doing big things. He doesn't have to do a lot more to make her happy. Sometimes he can actually do fewer big things and more little things and completely turn a relationship around.

It is action that sweeps a woman off her feet, but she is not dependent on a man's doing big things.

Some women do want men to do the big things. But once a woman discovers the little things a man can provide on a consistent basis, she begins to discover how important the little expressions of caring and support are. Most women already know this. It is men who think they have to have more, do more, and achieve more.

WHAT WOMEN REALLY WANT

Even when a woman complains in a relationship that she wants more, what she is really wanting more of is communication, caring, and understanding. When a man hears that she is upset about little things, he immediately and mistakenly assumes that she doesn't appreciate the big things he provides. He then concludes that he must do even bigger things to make her happy: He must make more money, plan a great vacation, buy a house, and so on.

On Mars a man thinks like this: If I do something really good and helpful for another person, then as an expression of her appreciation she will overlook any little mistakes I make. When a man gets involved with a woman, if she complains about the little stuff, he assumes she is not appreciating the big stuff. He feels an even greater pressure to do bigger things, which causes him to ignore the little things even more.

When a woman complains about the little stuff, a man assumes she is not appreciating the big stuff.

When a woman complains about the little stuff, it is really because for her the little stuff is just as important as the big stuff. Instead of resisting and misinterpreting this female tendency, a man can greatly benefit from it. If he wants to please and fulfill his partner, then he shouldn't focus so much on the big stuff. He should focus more on doing little things.

For a woman the little stuff is just as important as the big stuff.

Pleasing a woman is easier than most men could ever imagine. It is actually quite a relief for a man to understand that a woman can really love and appreciate him for the little things he does. Being appreciated for the little things can actually free a man from the pressures he feels from society to do more, achieve more, and have more. These are some examples of the little things that score big on Venus.

LITTLE WAYS TO SCORE BIG POINTS WITH A WOMAN

Be affectionate and touch her several times a day.

Listen with interest when she talks.

Plan ahead and schedule regular romantic dates or getaways.

Give her little compliments.

Bring her flowers.

Carry things for her.

Help her with her responsibilities when she is tired.

Offer to do helpful things without her having to ask.

Write her little notes occasionally to leave a message.

Encourage her to take time for herself.

It is not the big things that keep a relationship from working, it is the little things. Although couples may get caught up fighting about the big things, it is really the successful delivery of the little things that allows a woman to give the man the love he needs to keep giving of himself.

19

FINDING BALANCE

After a breakup or divorce, a man will often judge his ex-partner for the way she is dealing with the breakup. While he feels a need to pull away from relationships, she may become more active by dating around. To discover that she is busy dating may be hurtful to him, particularly if he feels rejected. A greater understanding of what women need may help him not to take her new interests so personally.

A man will tend to misinterpret a woman's behavior because his needs after a breakup are different. If he has given too much of himself and feels rejected, then to restore balance in his life he may want to isolate himself for a while. Using this time alone, he can properly explore and process his feelings and regain a healthy sense of independence, self-sufficiency, and autonomy. This is a time for him to be alone and to spend time with family and friends. It is not a time for him to get involved in a committed relationship. By pulling away in this manner, he will be on the right track for him.

Taking time to be alone allows a man
to feel his independence,
self-sufficiency, and autonomy.

Meanwhile a woman has a different need in the process of getting better. She finds balance by regaining a healthy sense of self-assurance, grace, and interdependence. If she has not been getting what she needs, she may want to get out and go on a vacation with a girlfriend. Behaviors that he might judge as selfish are exactly what she needs to be doing. It is also not wrong for her to act like a single woman and to enjoy the company of men. The reassurance she gets from the affections and interest of many men will assist her in the healing process.

A woman is able to find balance often by getting away from her responsibilities and letting others take care of her needs. Although it is fine for her to enjoy the interest of other men, ideally she must be careful not to get seriously involved with one partner. Caring for her partner's needs in an exclusive relationship may pull her away from taking time to feel, recognize, and nurture her own needs. The best advice is for her to date around with many men and avoid making a commitment.

SLEEPING AROUND FOR MEN

After a painful breakup or divorce, men and women may equally feel the need to sleep around in order to feel good about themselves. When this is the case, both must be careful not to move right into another committed relationship. After a loss of love, we need time to focus on our own needs and not the needs of another. Before we become exclusive again, we need first to heal our feelings of loss.

Sleeping around or regular sexual release can help a man continue to stay in touch with the feelings he needs to heal. Without sexual release, it is easy for men to get caught up in their minds unaware of their feelings of loss. For some men it is only by means of sex or sexual release that they can get out of their heads and feel the emptiness of their lives. After experiencing sexual release with a partner or alone in a shower, it is important for a man to take some time to feel the four healing emotions. The ideal time to process his feelings is actually after a sexual release.

Unless he consciously uses sex as a way to connect with his feelings, a man may unknowingly use sexual release as a way of avoiding his feelings. Any natural function in excess can become an addiction that leads us away from our feelings. For example, too much sleep, work, or food can also numb our pain and prevent us from feeling and healing our loss. Sex, like any other natural function, can either help us get in touch with our feelings or push them away. Moderation in sexual release for men and women is an important key in the process of healing.

SLEEPING AROUND FOR WOMEN

Women are more naturally inclined to be in touch with their feelings and are not as dependent on having a sexual release. Sex and romance for a woman can help her to rebuild her self-esteem after feeling ignored or unloved in a relationship. It is important for a woman to feel a man's desire to sustain a healthy level of self-esteem. When a woman is involved in an exclusive relationship and her partner loses interest in her, it is almost inevitable that her self-esteem weakens. Dating around and even sleeping around if she wishes can assist her in feeling good about herself once again.

Sex ideally should be an expression of feeling good and having something to share. A woman should not offer herself sexually in hopes of winning a man's commitment. This is a big mistake that can cause her much pain. Sex on the rebound should only be experienced to feel good and to create some connection to soothe her loneliness. A woman must be careful not to use sex as a way to become more seriously involved with a man. If she is serious about an involvement, then she should deliberately put sex off until she has healed her heart. If a woman is having sex expecting more from a man, she is setting herself up to be hurt.

THE PURSUIT OF SEX

Sex in itself is innocent as long as it is between two consenting adults. Yet sometimes the pursuit of sex can interfere with the healing process. The focus of getting sex may take us away from recognizing the true source of our pain. In our search for a sexual partner, we become overly concerned with how much sex we should be getting. When the pursuit of sex itself has become a source of pain, it is not healthy.

In this case, rather than remain frustrated by the pursuit of sex, we should take matters into our own hands, to stay on our healing track. By simply experiencing sexual release on our own without depending on a partner, we can take some private time to feel and heal our feelings of loss. After feeling better, we can move on to nurturing our other important needs for friendship, fun, self-reflection, and productive work. By regularly releasing our sexual tension, we are free from being preoccupied with sex and we have time to nurture our other needs as well.

Sexual release is only one of many needs. It is important that we do not deny it or obsess over it. Balance and moderation is always the best medicine. Good time sex with a partner or sexual release on our own is often mistakenly associated with guilt and shame. This is because after a sexual release our unresolved feelings come up. For example, if we are suppressing feelings of shame, sadness, and emptiness, these feelings automatically come up after a sexual release. If we do not understand this healing process, we mistakenly associate these negative feelings with the act of sexual release.

After a sexual release alone or with a partner, we may have bad feelings. Ideally we should then say to ourselves, "Okay, now I have the opportunity to feel and heal the emotions that are coming up. I am feeling bad not because I just did something bad. I am feeling bad because of my breakup; my unresolved feelings are coming up. I am experiencing the feelings of my past." By linking the feelings that come up with the past and practicing the feeling better technique, the healing process can begin.

Sexual release is not bad in itself, but it does open us up to facing our unresolved negative feelings. If we are suppressing feelings that make us feel bad, then after a sexual release those feelings will come up. To heal our hearts, it is important that we clearly recognize that sexual release is innocent and natural. It simply connects us to our natural feeling state, and suddenly we are faced with all our unresolved feelings.

Without an understanding of how to process the unresolved feelings that come up after sex, sexual release will leave us feeling bad, instead of making us feel good. Unless you are willing to apply the processing techniques in this book, sexual release is not recommended. It will just bring up the pain of our unresolved feelings again and again until we become numb to them through repression. If you are able to process the natural healing emotions that come up, then sexual release becomes an easy way to connect with and experience your healing emotions.

20

PICKING THE RIGHT WOMAN

One of the ways a man starting over pushes love out of his life is by not being able to make up his mind. He has difficulty picking one woman. He will start many relationships, but he never completes any. He may be dating three or more women simultaneously. When he thinks about making a commitment to one, he can't make up his mind because he suddenly begins thinking of all the good qualities of the other women he has been with.

For some men settling down
feels like settling for less.

One partner will seem good, but then he will move on to another. Every time he gets close to one, a past partner seems more desirable. He goes back to a past partner but then inevitably a new woman comes along and seems more desirable. In this way he keeps moving back to a past relationship and then ahead to a new one.

He can't make a commitment because no one is good enough. He thinks about all the good qualities of each woman, and he wants a composite of them all. The more women he dates, the more unrealistic his expectations become, the more difficult it is for him to decide. He cannot open himself to appreciating one relationship fully because he still holds on to his past.

A man thinks about all the good
qualities of each woman he has dated
and then wants a composite of them all.

This limiting pattern can often be handled best by simply changing the way he dates. When a man can't settle down, he either has unresolved past feelings or simply too many sexual partners. Sometimes by maintaining many sexual partners it is practically impossible to recognize a soul mate. The necessary conditions are not present for a man to recognize partner A as a soul mate, if he had just had sex with partner B within a three-month period. It is fine to have a series of sexual partners to help him connect with his feelings, but when he is ready to find a soul mate, he needs to slow down and give each relationship a chance.

It takes a consistent and monogamous blending of energies to recognize a soul mate. To know if he wants to share his life with a woman, a man's love for a woman must have a chance to grow. A particular bonding has to take place before a man can just "know" and be satisfied. If he has had sex with another woman during the bonding period, the bond breaks and he has to start over.

It takes a consistent and
monogamous blending of energies
to recognize a soul mate.

Without at least several months of exclusivity, it is impossible for a man to really know. He will just continue bouncing back and forth between desiring woman A and woman B. He will be caught up in his mind trying to figure who is right for him instead of knowing who is right from his heart and soul.

To end this cycle, he needs to pick one partner and temporarily forget the others. His objective is to pursue one relationship to its conclusion. He must be very careful to remain sexually exclusive with one and not even flirt with a new candidate. He can't even take numbers for the future.

During this time, it is normal to go through a period of feeling as if the grass is greener elsewhere. This time, instead of pursuing other interests, he must remain true. At this point, he may even lose all attraction for woman A. He should still stay with her for several more months. He needs to allow his sexual needs to recycle.

When a man has difficulty making
a commitment, it is common for him
to temporarily lose his feelings of
sexual attraction.

If he finds that his attraction for her comes back, then he will want to continue. If his sexual feelings don't come back, then he needs to end the relationship once and for all. It may also be that his sexual feelings remain strong, but after remaining true, he is able to recognize that she is not right for him.

In completing this relationship, he needs to be clear that he will not return. He then needs to heal any feelings that come up. If he wants to date around, that is fine, but before he makes a commitment again with a woman, he must sign off on any other women.

Before having sex he should set a standard. He must be at least committed to an exclusive relationship that feels as if she could be the one. He doesn't have to know for sure, but he should stop if he knows the woman he is sleeping with is not the one. It is a complete waste of his time and counterproductive for him to be intimate and have sex with a partner if she is definitely not the one.

By changing his dating patterns, this man will discover that he does have the ability to settle down and pick just one partner. By taking the time to do it right, he will not be plagued by doubts in the future. He will not feel as if he is missing out. Instead, he will feel that if he doesn't make a commitment he will miss out.

21

LEARNING TO SAY GOOD-BYE

While some men have difficulty saying yes to a relationship, others have difficulty saying no. After the loss of love, they get involved with a woman, but as they begin to recognize that she is not the one, they are unable to leave. She loves him, and he can't bear to hurt her by rejecting her.

It is very common for second marriages not to work out for this reason. A man gets involved right away, they become intimate, and they get married. They are both swept away by his impulsive neediness. He must have her now. They must get married right away. They cannot wait. Whenever we are this impulsive about getting married or becoming intimate, it is usually a mistake.

Second marriages commonly
don't work out because they are
rebound relationships.

Once he is married, his doubts begin to come up and he feels trapped. He wakes up from the dreamy state of infatuation and discovers that his partner is not the woman of his dreams. He is caught in a very painful situation. To be true to himself, he needs to leave. When they break up after getting married, the pain and hurt is unfortunately much greater than if he had rejected her before getting married. The longer he waits, the more painful and complicated it will be.

A man can spare himself and his partner this added pain by not getting married. Even better, he should not make any commitments right away. He needs to give himself time to be free, time to be by himself, and then plenty of time to date many women. By dating around, he will successfully prepare himself to find the right woman at the right time. After sex, he must be careful to process the feelings that come up.

When a man can't say no to a woman because he doesn't want to hurt her, there is an inner reason. This tendency comes from unresolved feelings of hurt within himself. If he has been hurt by someone who rejected him, then he doesn't want to hurt another in this same way. The inability to end a relationship is a clear sign that he still has work to do on his own hurt before he is ready to get involved. By eventually forgiving the person who hurt him, he will then be able to leave a relationship without the burden of feeling guilty.

WRITING A GOOD-BYE LETTER

Guilt or no guilt, if he needs to get out of a relationship he should do it. It is really the best gift he can give the woman he is afraid of hurting. If a man doesn't feel comfortable ending a relationship, he can write out what he wants to say and then read his feelings to her. It can be as simple as this example:

Dear _____,

I want you to know that I love you and care for you, but I do not feel that I should be in a relationship right now. I have not given myself enough time to get over my last relationship. I realize that I need to give myself time to date many women before making a commitment as I have done with you.

It is hard for me to say this, because I don't want to say or do anything that would hurt. Yet I must do this for myself. I feel sad that our relationship is over.

I am afraid that I will say this the wrong way and hurt you. I don't want to hurt you. I know that you love me and so I know this will probably hurt you a lot. I am sorry that I cannot give you what you want or protect you from this pain. I clearly know that I need to end this relationship.

Thank you for the good times. I will always remember the special moments and love that we have shared. You are a wonderful person and I trust that you will find the right person for you.

Love, _____

After writing out his thoughts, feelings, and clear intentions, he can then read his letter to his partner. It will not feel right if he just mails it and doesn't meet with her. A conversation after the letter is very important so that she feels her reactions are heard. He must be careful to not weaken his resolve. He must stick to his intention to end the relationship. He must be loving but firm.

She will ask, "Why?" The answer to this question can only be "I love you and I have realized that you are not the right one for me. If you are not right for me, then I know I am not the right person for you."

If he gets involved in petty reasons, then she will ask for him to give her another chance or to give the relationship more time. She may promise to change or ask him to change. This is all a diversion. The real reason to end a relationship is the same reason that we would plan to get married. In our hearts we just know it. When our love is unconditional, there are no reasons. The reasons we may feel to be with someone or not to be with someone are all secondary to a feeling in our hearts that says yea or nay.

Even when this man is not on the rebound, he may still have difficulty ending an intimate relationship. If a man knows for sure that the person he is dating is not the right person, then he could write a letter like this one and then read it:

Dear _____,

I want you to know that I love you and care for you very much. I am writing this letter to you because it is hard for me to say these words to you. I do not want to hurt you. You are such a special woman. You deserve to be loved and adored. I have realized that even though I love you very much, you are not the one for me. I want to break up.

I am sorry if this hurts a lot. I want you to be happy and fulfilled, and I clearly know that I am not the man to do it. I trust that you will find the love that you deserve, and that I will move on to find the right person for me.

The time I have spent with you has been very special, and I will always remember it.

Love, _____

Breaking up for some men is very difficult. By overcoming this challenge, they are then able to forgive all the women in their past who may have rejected them. Saying no to a relationship that is clearly not right for us is powerful preparation for being able to find and recognize the right person in the future.

22

SELF-DESTRUCTIVE TENDENCIES

When a man is unable to feel and heal his feeling of loss, he may become caught in the grip of self-destructive tendencies. To the extent that he cannot deal with his feelings of hurt constructively, he will tend to hurt himself. He may get caught by addictive substances, he may run away and start a new life, he may risk his life, he may throw away his life force, or he may even try to take his life. As he loses control, his life will continue to spiral downward until he bottoms out and seeks help.

Without a clear understanding of an alternative way of dealing with his pain, a man will not reach out for support. Eventually, as his life gets worse and worse, he may realize that he can't help himself alone. Many people believe that until a man bottoms out in this way he cannot get better.

This does not have to be the case. If a man has a choice, he doesn't need to bottom out. By understanding the healing process, a man in need can use his reasoning powers to recognize the value of support and how to go about getting it.

If a man recognizes that he has a choice,
then he doesn't need to bottom out.

Even if he were to start practicing the healing processes in this book on his own, he could begin to get better. As his heart begins to open again, he will be able to recognize the value of group support as well. He must realize that the reason he feels self-destructive tendencies is that some feelings are being repressed. Without the help of others, it is almost impossible to recover fully.

INTERVENTION

When a loved one is under the grip of self-destructive tendencies, there are many expert counselors who can help with an intervention. Even if a man is not reaching out, he can be helped though intervention. Although a man must be responsible for his cure, to help him overcome self-destructive tendencies, his family and friends can make a big difference.

It is not appropriate to lecture him on what he should or should not do, but it is appropriate for friends and family to let him know how his behavior affects them. It is also a good time for family members to do the feeling better exercises and to read out loud their letters expressing feelings of anger, sadness, fear, sorrow, love, understanding, desire, and trust. Letting him know how they feel without telling him what he has to do can be very healing and empowering.

To intervene it is not appropriate to tell a man what to do, but it is helpful to share how he makes you feel.

By hearing the honest feelings of the people he is hurting, he will find the strength to make the changes he needs to make. If he thinks that no one is being affected by his decline, then it is easier for him to slide downward into a pit of despair. Men are always inspired when they are needed. Hearing the feelings of others can wake a man up to his ability to overcome his adversity. Although he may not like it, later on he will thank his friends and family for their support.

HEALING HIS PAST

Self-destructive tendencies occur to the extent that a man has a tendency to repress certain feelings. When men or women display self-destructive tendencies, it is important for them to recognize that they cannot get better alone. Their condition requires the assistance of outside support. If outside conditions in his childhood have repressed his feelings, then it will take outside conditions to open him up to his feelings. This is when a man needs a counselor or support group the most.

Repressed feelings cause
self-destructive tendencies.

If he has been raised in a punishing environment, then he will be particularly self-destructive. When he experiences the humiliation of failure, he then punishes himself. To eventually break free of this punishing tendency, he needs to remember times when he was punished or afraid of being punished. By processing and healing unresolved feelings from that time in his life, he can break the pattern.

RUNNING AWAY THROUGH ALCOHOL AND DRUGS

To make his life bearable, a man may run away from his pain through excessive use of alcohol and drugs. If he already has a pattern of drinking or taking drugs, then during a healing crisis this habit is hard to resist. By creating an altered state of mind, he is able to avoid his true feelings. Mind-altering substances temporarily numb our painful feelings, but they grip the mind and body into a state of dependency.

We are most vulnerable to addictive substances right after a loss. When our heart is in pain, our body is in pain. To cope with that pain, the body begins to produce natural endorphins to relieve the pain.

The grieving processes described in this
book stimulate the natural production
of pain-reducing endorphins.

Drugs and alcohol will also stimulate the body to
release pain-reducing endorphins. The problem
with outside stimulants is that the body stops producing the endorphins on its own. When we are not
high or under the influence, the body experiences
the incredible agony of withdrawal. It is extremely
painful because the body has stopped generating
the normal feel-good endorphins that allow our
hearts to open and our minds to be at peace.

By avoiding addictive substances, a man may
have to face his pain, but the pain will be much less
than the physical and emotional agony of withdrawal. By checking into a detox program or joining an AA group, he has a chance of getting the
support he needs without having to bottom out.

RUNNING AWAY IN HIS CAR

When a man's ability to feel his emotions is
blocked, he may feel a tremendous numbness or
lifelessness. To feel alive again, he may feel an urge
to get away. He may just get in his car and drive
away into the sunset. He has no idea where he
wants to go, he just knows he wants to get away.

Driving away makes him feel as if he can leave
his problems and pain behind. Eventually he discovers that his problems are like his shadow:

They don't go away or disappear when he leaves town or changes locations. Although he may find relief, he must be careful that he doesn't burn any bridges or drive away from the valuable support of friends and family.

Our unresolved feelings are like a shadow: They don't go away when we leave town.

As long as he is driving safely, and if he likes to drive, then great. Instead of driving away and staying away, he should eventually come back. To heal his heart he needs to face his feelings and not run away. Leaving behind everyone who loves him is another self-destructive tendency.

A man runs away because he feels unworthy of being seen and supported. By facing his friends, he will learn one of the most incredibly healing lessons of a lifetime. He will be surprised that he will be loved even when he feels most unworthy of love.

RISKING HIS LIFE

Sometimes when a man is repressing his feelings the only way he can feel alive is to risk his life or be a daredevil in some way. After a loss, he may go off to climb a mountain or race a car. As long as he remains reasonably safe, there is nothing wrong with taking risks. People do it every day. Taking time off to climb a mountain or go into the wilderness is good in that it may help him to feel more independent and autonomous again.

When a man risks his life doing something, it forces him to focus all his energies into a survival mode. When he is concerned about life-and-death issues, he temporarily disconnects from his need to love and be loved. Suddenly the pain of losing love is insignificant compared to the danger of losing his life. To stay alive, he must keep his mind completely focused in the moment. During that time, he feels the exhilaration of fully being in touch with his feelings.

The pain of losing love is automatically suppressed when we face danger.

Although this is a positive escape, it does not heal his hurt feelings nor does it correct his tendency to repress feelings. Being in the moment frees us from our past temporarily, but it doesn't heal our past. As soon as we are not in danger, our unresolved feelings come up to be healed. Before rushing off to another risky adventure, he needs to take time to process his feelings.

Often people wonder why therapy focuses so much on past issues if the real goal is to be in the moment. Looking at the past is important because it is the incomplete experiences of the past that actually pull us out of the present moment. When we take time to listen to our past, then it doesn't invade the present. The ideal is to be fully present in the moment, feeling fully alive and in touch with our feelings without having to be in danger.

LOSING HIS LIFE ENERGY

When a man's heart is closed, he may become sexually obsessed with women for whom he does not feel any affection. The energy that is blocked in his heart seeks release through the outlet of sex. Sex allows him to begin feeling again.

A man can reduce emotional tension he feels by releasing his sexual life energy. With intense sexual stimulation, he is able to experience a momentary release. Although the process of dissipating life energy through loveless sex may feel good, he does not feel good afterwards. Although he feels relief from tension, he senses that he has lost something as well. This feeling of loss is not because he had loveless sex, but is actually his unresolved past feeling of loss.

Loveless sex may feel good,
but afterwards a man feels
empty and spent.

When a man is repressing his painful feelings, he may hunger for the pleasure of sex. He will experience a strong attraction to prostitutes, pornography, and excessive masturbation. He will be attracted to women in whom he is not interested in pursuing beyond a sexual relationship. He is particularly sexually attracted when there is no chance of intimacy. To heal his heart, after such encounters he needs to process and heal the painful feelings of shame, loss, and emptiness that come up. To avoid excessive sexual stimulation, cold showers, exercise, eating, classes, and non-sexual movies are helpful. More than one ejaculation a day could indicate a sexual addiction.

TAKING HIS LIFE

The ultimate self-destructive tendency is a man's attempt to commit suicide. While more women attempt suicide, more men actually succeed. A man considers suicide when life becomes unbearable. Often it is the shame associated with failure that makes him want to die. He would rather die than face his family and friends and admit his inadequacy. He can't accept their support because he feels unworthy of it.

A man may kill himself because he doesn't know what else to do. If he cannot save face, then he must die. Women commit suicide when the pain of not getting what they need is so great that they can't bear it and don't know what else to do. Often a woman will let others know that she wants to commit suicide as a way to express her need for help.

To save face after the humiliation of failure, a man may feel he must die.

When a man commits suicide, it is because he doesn't know what else to do and he believes that his presence will only make matters worse for everyone. He would rather die than face the consequences of failure. He can't bear the thought of disappointing the ones he loves. When he begins to think that by staying alive he will make matters worse, killing himself becomes a way he can help to solve the problem he has caused.

A general reason for suicide that applies to men and women is that we seek to die as a way to stop feeling our pain. We want to leave our pain behind.

Underneath a death urge is really the desire to be free of pain, to be happy again and to find peace.

A way to change a suicidal tendency is to acknowledge the feeling that "I want to die." Then go a little deeper and ask, "Why do I want to die?" The answer will always be life affirming. It comes out something like this: "I want be free of pain, I want to stop hurting, I want to leave all this behind, I want to be free, I want to be happy, I want peace of mind, I want to live."

After getting in touch with these positive intentions behind our death urge, a person can begin to process the four healing emotions. By connecting with our desire to live, it is then easier to connect with our feelings of anger, sadness, fear, and sorrow. While this can be done alone, until we are proficient, it is good to share these feelings with a counselor to assist you.

23

FINDING THE POWER TO PROVIDE

After the loss of love, a man is faced with all kinds of feelings of insecurity. Although he may be very confident in his work, when faced with having to date again, it is natural to have fears. Regardless of how his relationship ended, it is embarrassing and frightening to start dating again.

When a man is over forty, he may feel very awkward. If he has been married for a while, he may not know where to start, where to meet people. Dating customs have changed dramatically. Women today have new needs and different expectations. It will take some time for him to find his confidence and comfort with the dating process.

Dating customs have changed
dramatically; it is much more
complicated than before.

By being there for himself and not rushing into having a committed relationship on the rebound, a man will gradually find an easy stride. Eventually he will develop an inner confidence and an awareness of his power to provide. When he begins to feel he has the power to sweep a woman off her feet, then he will be most successful in finding the right person for him.

If his primary goal is to find a sexual partner and have sex, then he postpones the opportunity to experience increasing success in the dating process. By discovering and experiencing that there is much more than sex to be gained by getting to know someone, his ability to acclimate to his new single status is much easier.

DATING YOUNGER WOMEN

When a man is over forty and he is not yet feeling comfortable being single, he will automatically be attracted to younger women. Their youth and lack of experience makes him suddenly feel more competent and powerful. When a woman is in her twenties, she is quite often attracted to an older, more powerful man. He is more mature than men her age. This can be very appealing for her, particularly if she is feeling a little insecure and looking for someone to help her.

There is nothing wrong with dating a younger woman. It can actually bring life back into him. By connecting with younger women, he automatically feels younger and more powerful. This can best be viewed as a phase, a supportive opportunity to connect with a part of his past. Often, when a man is young, he doesn't have the confidence of an older man. When an older man can feel young again and also have his confidence, it can be very freeing and fulfilling.

One of the problems with dating younger women is that as they get older things change. As a woman gets closer to her thirties, her hormones begin to change. She is not as accommodating as before. She feels a greater need to be herself and doesn't bend her will as easily to a male partner.

> As a woman gets closer to her thirties, her hormones begin to change and she becomes less accommodating.

Another possible problem is attraction. It is hard to stay interested in someone who has a different level of maturity. Unless he is very young at heart and she is more mature at heart, after the initial rush of hormones, they will lose interest in each other. To make sure he is getting involved with the right woman for him, a man needs to be careful about getting married right away to a younger woman. He needs to take time to develop his power to provide and make sure he is attracted to the right woman for him.

FAILURE TO PERFORM SEXUALLY

While starting over, almost every man will experience some inability to perform sexually. He often panics and thinks something is wrong. Nothing is wrong. It is just his body telling him that he is not yet ready to become sexual. His body is telling him to slow down.

Even if he feels a sexual hunger, when the opportunity presents itself, he will either not be able to get an erection, lose his erection before intercourse, experience a premature ejaculation, or have an erection but not be able to come. When any of the above symptoms occur he mistakenly assumes that something is wrong. Instead he needs to recognize that he is just not ready to go that far.

When a man's body fails to
perform sexually, it is a signal
telling him to slow down.

When he is still holding on to some hurt, he cannot give himself sexually to a woman he cares for. He may perform great with a prostitute or alone in the shower, but when he is with a woman that he cares about his body will not perform. Trying to make it happen before he is ready will only complicate the process.

Based on sex not working in the past, his performance anxiety automatically increases the next time he tries. It is best that he realize his body is sending him a message. As he heals his heart and begins to experience his natural power to provide, then his full sexual abilities will be available to him.

RESCUING WOMEN

When a man is not yet feeling his power to provide, he will often be attracted to a woman in need. If he can come rescue her then he suddenly feels powerful again. Though this feels good, he must be careful. He may become dependent on her to feel confident and powerful. It is best that he first feel his power to provide and then get more intimately involved.

Depending on a woman to feel powerful is not real power. Her neediness temporarily frees him from feeling his powerlessness. When he has the means to solve her problems, he may immediately feel turned on. If he has been in pain, he will suddenly feel better. This kind of romance, although passionate, often doesn't last.

When a man has the means
to solve a woman's problems,
he may immediately feel
turned on by her.

Once she is no longer desperate and feeling her need for him to rescue her, the attraction lessens. He or she may discover that they are not right for each other. His attraction is often just based on a desire to be helpful and the pleasure of feeling powerful again. A man can get this same rush of power by helping her and not getting involved sexually. Then it is easy to walk away in case they are not right for each other.

FINDING A NURTURING WOMAN

Another common attraction a man experiences when he is in the process of recovering his power is a temporary attraction to nurturing women. A nurturing woman helps him to feel the wounds of his childhood. Once his wounds are healed, he will often discover that she is not the right pick for him.

When a man has unresolved childhood issues, he may be drawn to a woman who will comfort him as if he were a little boy. He will want her to treat him the way he would have wanted his mother to treat him. Once his pain is comforted, he will lose his attraction. At best his attraction will be on and off.

When a man is attracted to a nurturing woman during the healing process, that attraction is often short-lived.

After they consummate the relationship, it becomes even more confusing. He will automatically begin to project his unresolved feelings on her. To the extent that he feels the need for her to play the role of his mother, his unresolved feelings from childhood become projected onto her. What he felt about his mother, he will begin to feel about her.

For example, if he has unresolved issues of anger and hurt, then in his adult relationship he will become overly sensitive and hurt by the things she says and does. He will overreact with anger. It is hard enough to have a relationship in present time without inviting in the past. Before a man makes a commitment, he must be careful that he is not seek- ing a nurturing mother to heal his wounds.

Sex during the healing process
intensifies the tendency to
project our past feelings.

To have a sexual relationship with a nurturing woman and make a lasting commitment during the healing process, puts a strain on the relation- ship and obstructs the natural healing process. By depending too much on a woman in this way, a man will also delay his ability to feel independent and powerful again. Although this relationship may bring him comfort and healing, he will begin to feel confined.

If a man feels attracted to nurturing women during his process of healing, he should turn to a female therapist. She will be able to give him the nurturing he seeks and he will also be able to grow in independence and power. In this way he can take the time he needs to recover his power before making a commitment.

When a man needs a mothering
woman, he is wise to seek out a
female therapist instead.

In each of these examples, a man is attracted to a woman or situation in which he feels powerful. There is nothing limiting about his tendency as long as he is careful to avoid a lasting commitment during the healing crisis.

By leaving commitment out of the equation, he is free to experience his power to provide without feeling too attached. Although it requires restraint, a man is greatly empowered by giving to others without intimately depending on them. A wonderful confidence will eventually emerge that will not only make the dating process fun, but also prepare him for the right relationship. Aware of his power to provide, he will be able to sustain passion for a lifetime.

It is a great empowerment for a man to experience free sexual expression without having to make a lasting commitment. To experience a woman's sexual favors without conditions helps him to feel and heal his wounded feelings of attachment. Having healed his heart, he is then ready to find love and make a commitment.

AFTERWORD

FACING A FORK IN THE ROAD

When starting over, both men and women stand at a fork in the road. One road leads upward to light, love, and hope. The other road leads down into darkness, despair, and emptiness. The upward road starts out difficult. It requires feeling our pain and having to learn new ways of relating. It requires challenging ourselves to be the best we can be. The other road starts out easier, but eventually becomes more painful and difficult. It promises relief, but does not heal our hearts. It does not bring us back home.

By taking the risk to love again, you become not only stronger but more loving as well. By rising to the challenge of healing your heart, you will move on to find an even greater love. With a heart full of love, you will express your highest potential while also fulfilling your soul's deepest purpose: to love and be loved.

You are not the only beneficiary of this grace. Your children benefit as well. As long as their parents are in pain, a part of them will be hurting. Parents often wonder what they can do for their children. The greatest gift they can ever give is to be examples of love and healing. As you heal your heart, your children automatically grow in love. As you heal and release your pain it lightens their load as well.

The pain you do not heal, you leave behind for your children to carry. When your load becomes heavy and you feel like giving up, remember that you are also doing it for them. You are not just helping yourself, but carrying them out of harm's way into the safety and warmth of love.

By taking the time to read this book, you have expressed your commitment to completing your healing journey and to coming back home to your heart. Although this may be the most painful time of your entire life, you will look back and be thankful for the gifts your healing brings. Through healing your broken heart, you will become stronger than ever before. This pain will pass, and you will experience a new life of greater love, understanding, and compassion beyond what you could ever imagine.

Even if it has been many years since your loss, it is never too late to turn around, heal your heart, and then move on to find true and lasting love. If you've already made some of the mistakes mapped out in *Mars and Venus Starting Over*, you still have the choice to find love again.

LEARNING TO LET GO

Richard had been married for twenty-three years before he was divorced. He had married young. After twenty-three years, he realized that he was with the wrong woman for him. Instead of taking time to heal his heart, he went on to begin many relationships. He made almost every mistake in this book.

As he would commit to one woman, suddenly his doubts would come up and then he would date another. After three years of becoming intimately involved with six women, he couldn't make up his mind and commit. Each woman had some good qualities that he was hoping to find. To pick one meant he had to let go of the others. Rather than pick one, he even considered giving up the whole idea of being in a relationship.

After taking a Mars-Venus workshop, Richard was able to start again, this time more successfully. He realized that he couldn't let go of his new relationships because he hadn't yet let go of his wife. By healing his unresolved feelings toward his ex-partner, he was able to change his dating experience. By completing his marriage, he was eventually able to complete his other relationships as well.

A year later, he found the perfect woman for him and went on to experience true and lasting love. When he was really ready to get involved, he discovered that the right woman for him actually lived down the block from him. This time it was not difficult at all for him to make a commitment.

FINDING FORGIVENESS

Lucy had experienced a betrayal in her marriage. Her ex-husband had fallen in love with his secretary and left her. She was devastated. To rebuild her confidence, she began dating around. Although it felt good to be appreciated and adored, it was never enough. It couldn't be enough, because she was still being influenced by unresolved feelings about her marriage. She did not know how to process and heal her hurt feelings.

She eventually decided to focus on her career and her children and not be concerned with a relationship. Nine years later, she was reasonably content, but something was still missing. After taking a Mars-Venus workshop, she discovered that she was still holding on to unresolved hurt feelings. By learning to feel the four healing emotions, she was able to find forgiveness and experience a healthy desire for intimacy in her life.

Although Lucy thought she would never find love again, by taking the time to heal her heart, she realized that she had a choice. With this change in attitude, within six months she met a man who eventually turned out to be the perfect man for her. By healing her heart, she was able to start over and find lasting love.

CHOOSING TO LOVE AGAIN

Equipped with the simple insights of *Mars and Venus Starting Over,* you now have a choice which way you turn. You have a map to lead you on your journey. Like a wise teacher, I hope it helps you find the answers you seek; like a good friend, I hope it travels by your side. Like an angel from heaven, may it comfort you in your time of great need and remind you that you are loved, that you are not forgotten, that your prayers are being answered.

On your journey back home, you will find the support you need to continue making the best choices. At each new fork in the road, as you choose to heal your heart, remember that you are bringing God's love back into this world. Choose to love not just for yourself but for your children, your friends, and even the world. Always remember that your love is needed. Thank you for sharing your journey with me, and thank you for letting me make a difference in your life.

If you like what you just read
and want to learn more...

Call our representatives, Mars-Venus Institute, twenty-four hours a day, seven days a week, toll free, at 1-888-INFO-MVI (1-888-463-6684) or visit John Gray's website at www.marsvenus.com for information on the following subjects:

MARS-VENUS SPEAKERS BUREAU

More than 500,000 individuals and couples around the world have already benefited from John Gray's relationship seminars. We invite and encourage you to share with John this safe, insightful and healing experience. Because of the popularity of his seminars and talks, Dr. Gray has developed programs for presentations by individuals he has personally trained. These seminars are available for both the general public as well as private corporate functions. Please call for current schedules and booking information.

MARS-VENUS WORKSHOPS

Mars-Venus Workshops are interactive classes based on the bestselling books *Men Are from Mars, Women Are from Venus* and *Mars and Venus on a Date* by Dr. John Gray. His personally trained instructors facilitate these workshops worldwide. While millions of people have improved their relationships by reading these books, taking a Mars-Venus Workshop will deepen your understanding of this material and permanently alter your instinctive behavior while you participate in a fun, interactive, non-confrontational, and "male-friendly" class.

The Mars-Venus Institute also trains those interested in presenting Mars-Venus Workshops in their own community. You can call the Mars-Venus Institute toll free at 1-888-INFO-MVI (1-888-463-6684). If you are out of the USA, call 415-389-6857, or check us out on our website: www.marsvenusinstitute.com.

MARS & VENUS COUNSELING CENTERS

In response to the thousands of requests we have received for licensed professionals that use the Mars/Venus principles in their practice, John Gray has established the Mars & Venus Counseling Centers and Counselor Training. Participants in this program have completed a rigorous study of John's work and have demonstrated a commitment to his valuable concepts. If you are interested in a referral to a counselor in your area call 1-800-649-4155. If you seek information about training as a Mars & Venus counselor or establishing a Mars & Venus Counseling Center, please call 1-800-735-6052.

Videos, Audiotapes and Books by John Gray

For further explorations of the wonderful world of Mars and Venus, see the descriptions that follow and call us to place an order for additional information.

Mars-Venus Institute
20 Sunnyside Avenue, A-130
Mill Valley, CA 94941
1-888-MARSVENUS (1-888-627-7836)

VIDEOS

JOHN GRAY TWO-PACK VHS VIDEOTAPE SERIES

In these five 2-pack VHS tape series, Dr. John Gray explains how differences between men and women—Martians and Venusians—can develop mutually fulfilling and loving relationships. Series includes:

MEN ARE FROM MARS, WOMEN ARE FROM VENUS

(2-Pack #1)

Tape #1:
Improving Communication
(60 mins.)

Tape #2:
How to Motivate the Opposite Sex
(56 mins.)

MARS AND VENUS IN THE BEDROOM

(2-Pack #2)

Tape #1:
Great Sex
(80 mins.)

Tape #2:
The Secrets of Passion
(47 mins.)

MARS AND VENUS TOGETHER FOREVER
Understanding the Cycles of Intimacy

(2-Pack #3)

Tape #1:
Men Are Like Rubber Bands
(45 mins.)

Tape #2:
Women Are Like Waves (62 mins.)

MARS AND VENUS ON A DATE

(2-Pack #4)

Tape #1:
Navigating the Five Stages of Dating
(57 mins.)

Tape #2:
The Secrets of Attraction (71 mins.)

MARS AND VENUS STARTING OVER

(2-Pack #5)

Tape #1:
Finding Love Again
(107 mins.)

Tape #2:
The Gift of Healing (105 mins.)

FOR ALL AGES AND STAGES OF RELATIONSHIPS...THERE IS HOPE.

MARS AND VENUS STARTING OVER

A Guide to Recreating a Loving and Lasting Relationship

Whether newly single after a death, a divorce or other serious break-up, women and men will find comforting and empowering advice on overcoming loss and gaining the confidence to engage in new relationships.

Hardcover,
0-06-017598-2 $25.00
Trade paperback,
0-06-093027-6 $14.00

Two audiocassettes,
read by the author (abridged)
0-694-51976-6 $18.00

Keep Passion Alive!

MARS AND VENUS IN THE BEDROOM

A Guide to Lasting
Romance and Passion

Hardcover
0-06-017212-6 $24.00
Trade paperback
0-06-092793-3 $13.00
Two audiocassettes (abridged)
1-55994-883-3 $18.00

Also available in Spanish:

**MARTE Y
VENUS EN
EL DORMITORIO**

Trade paperback
0-06-095180-X $11.00
Two audiocassettes (abridged)
0-694-51676-7 $18.00

The Keys to Making Love Last!

MARS AND VENUS TOGETHER FOREVER

A Practical Guide to Creating
Lasting Intimacy

Trade paperback
0-06-092661-9 $13.00
Mass market paperback
0-06-104457-1 $6.99

Also available in Spanish:

**MARTE Y VENUS
JUNTOS PARA
SIEMPRE**

Trade paperback
0-06-095236-9 $11.00

ALSO AVAILABLE:

THE MARS AND VENUS AUDIO COLLECTION

Contains one of each cassette:
Men Are from Mars, Women Are from Venus; What Your Mother Couldn't Tell You and Your Father Didn't Know; and
Mars and Venus in the Bedroom.

Three audiocassettes (abridged)
0-694-51589-2 $39.00

MEN, WOMEN AND RELATIONSHIPS

Making Peace with the Opposite Sex
Mass market paperback
0-06-101070-7 $6.99
One audiocassette (abridged)
0-694-51534-5 $12.00

WHAT YOU FEEL YOU CAN HEAL,

A Guide for Enriching Relationships
Two audiocassettes (abridged)
0-694-51613-9 $18.00